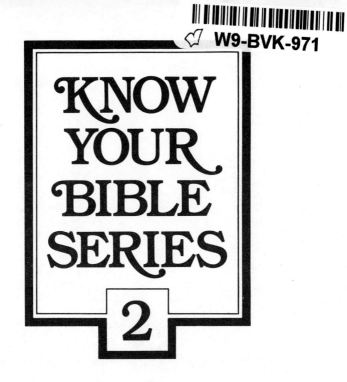

KNOW YOUR BIBLE SERIES

2

AMOS

HOSEA

ISAIAH

MICAH

ROY L. SMITH

ABINGDON PRESS
NASHVILLE

Amos, Hosea, Isaiah, Micah

No. 209137

Printed in U.S.A.

INTRODUCTION

To a vast multitude of Christians the utterances of the Old Testament prophets are almost meaningless because they know nothing of the historical and economic conditions out of which those devoted men spoke. But as we discover the facts with which they dealt, and measure them alongside facts in our own world with which we are painfully familiar, we begin to have the feeling that Amos, Hosea, Micah, and Isaiah are almost contemporaries.

Once we know the circumstances under which the prophets lived and labored, these ancient worthies emerge from the shadows as extremely practical men who lived on Main Street and who were immersed in the desperate struggles through which their neighbors passed. They cease to be starry-eyed dreamers, mysteriously predicting far-off events for the guidance of generations still unborn, and become flesh-and-blood heroes who warned and pleaded with their neighbors in behalf of justice, righteousness, and genuine piety.

Because of their faith, their true piety, and their insistence upon the priority of human rights, they are at home in every generation in which the struggle goes on in behalf of the common man. Their declaration of principles becomes the rallying cry of the crusaders of every century—those rare souls who love mercy, seek justice, and dream of a better world for plain people.

Hebrew prophets were not magicians who rubbed crystal balls and read strange secrets therefrom. Nor were they diviners who, by some weird legerdemain, conjured up visions of events that were still to come. Neither were they exotic souls who fell into trances and came back reporting hidden mysteries.

Rather, they were careful thinkers and profound students of their times who faced the facts of their day with a triumphant faith in a God of righteousness. They talked about those facts in terms of what they believed to be the mind of God. Always down to earth, forever honest, of astounding courage, usually in the minority, consumed with the passion of their convictions, they dared to claim that the words they spoke were words of God. They frankly asserted that they spoke in his behalf.

We do the prophets a serious injustice if we undertake to interpret them as mystics speaking for two ages and two civilizations at the same time. They were never such. There is no double meaning in their plainly spoken words. At all times they were bent on making plain the mind of God to a people who, according to their belief, were sinning against God. When they preached they had but one generation in mind—the one of which they were a part. Whatever message they may have for our generation lies in the eternal quality of the truth they spoke in their own day.

We will set out, then, to study the world's first great crisis in which the first great world state arose, and in doing so we will meet four towering personalities—all laymen—who were profoundly convinced that their messages were from God, and desperately desirous of seeing the nation conform to the will of God as they interpreted it.

ROY L. SMITH

Beginning Bible Study

1 **How should a student begin his study of the Bible?**

Ordinarily, in studying any book, we begin at the beginning, but in studying the Bible that does not mean beginning at the first page.

2 **Where then does the study of the Bible begin?**

The first books of the Bible to be completed in their present form were written in the midst of the world's first great political crisis and are the product of that event.

3 **Which books are they?**

Four books written by Hebrew prophets—Amos, Hosea, Isaiah, and Micah.

4 **What was that world crisis?**

It was a life-and-death struggle between two great empires of the ancient world (Egypt and Assyria) in which the mastery of the whole Eastern world was the prize at stake.

5 **When did this crisis occur?**

Just as it is true of any great event of history, its roots ran far back into the past. Several trends had been developing through at least a century, which came to a climax toward the close of the eighth century B.C., when the armies of Assyria took up the march and started on their long-anticipated campaign against Egypt.

6 **What part did the Hebrew kings and kingdoms play in the crisis?**

To arrive at any satisfactory understanding of the situation and of the roles played by the little states, it will be necessary to (1) restudy the circumstances under which the Hebrews settled in the Land of Promise, (2) survey the peculiar significance of the "Fertile Crescent," in the ancient world, and (3) review the history of the Hebrews from the time of their settlement of the land to the middle of the eighth century B.C., when the crisis was beginning to assume serious aspects.

7 Under what circumstances did the Hebrews enter the land?

According to the best opinion of American scholars, the Hebrews made their exodus from Egypt under the leadership of Moses about 1290 B.C. It was an extremely auspicious time for launching a new nation in the ancient East.

The Empire of Assyria, lying along the northern borders of Palestine and stretching away to the upper reaches of the Tigris and Euphrates valleys, had been a powerful and vigorous nation a few hundred years earlier; but in 1290 B.C. it was in a sorry state of decline, utterly unable to take any part in Palestinian politics.

Egypt, stretched out along the narrow green valley of the Nile, was also in a state of disorganization. There had been a time when it had held sway over a vast territory extending far to the north and east, but at the time of the Exodus its energies were so sapped by domestic difficulties that it had no power to interfere with the affairs of the small nations in the Land of Promise.

The presence of thousands of Hebrew aliens in the district of Goshen was a cause of great concern to the government of Egypt toward the close of the fourteenth century B.C. The province in which they lived, bordering as it did on Palestine, was on the Empire's eastern frontier and was certain to feel any blows which an invader might strike. This was a hazard which Egypt could not tolerate, and in an effort to protect the Empire's flank the Hebrews were degraded according to a methodical plan (Exodus 1:9-12).

In spite of the fact that the exodus of Hebrew slaves created a labor shortage for Egypt it was not an unmixed disaster, for it removed a dangerous element who could have been of very great help to an invading army. This may explain the comparative ease with which the nation made its escape.

Once out of Egypt with his charges, Moses spent forty years in the desert, training them in religion and government and finally molding them into something resembling a unity. But it is an impressive commentary on the times that they were able to fight their way into the Land of Promise and establish themselves without interference from any great power. Only in a day of political confusion could it have been done. The

6

Hebrews were beneficiaries of a world that was politically impotent.

8 What was the "Fertile Crescent"?

If the student will consult a good map of the East he will note that, beginning some little distance up the Mediterranean coast from the Nile delta, a fringe of fertile land appears. This is the western tip of an arc that has been known to history as the "Fertile Crescent." With this narrow strip as a starting point, it stretches away to the north and east, and then follows the gentle curve of the Tigris and Euphrates valleys down to the Persian Gulf in the general form of an inverted crescent enclosing the Arabian desert. In this friendly area the oldest known civilization on earth developed. Here one of the greatest empires of all time—the Assyrian—grew up, to be followed many years afterward by another, only slightly less powerful— the Babylonian.

The two great empires of the East came into existence (1) along the banks of the Nile in Africa and (2) in the upper regions of the Fertile Crescent in Asia. Between them the vast stretches of the Arabian desert lay like a sea of sand, with the narrow strip of fertile land along the Mediterranean coast forming the bridge across which commerce flowed. At one end of the bridge lay the Assyrian Empire, and at the other end the rich and voluptuous Egypt of the Nile.

Because of its peculiar setting this little bridge of land became one of the most vital and strategic bits of territory on the face of all the earth. Every trader, caravan, and army which traveled east or west, north or south, had to pass over it at one time or another. Every great intercontinental trade route crossed its plains. From the hills of Judah and from the cites of Israel the Hebrews watched the people of the earth pass their doors. Indeed, the world came and camped in their midst. It was impossible for them to live alone, or in peace. Every war in the world became theirs. No man in Palestine could think about politics without thinking in terms of world politics.

9 What was the history of the Hebrew settlement in Palestine?

The nomads of the desert had long battled along the frontier of the Fertile Crescent in an effort to fight their way in from the barren wastes to the fertile valleys where livings were easier and life was more settled. Thus the Hebrews were not the first ones to invade the land and to fight desperately with its inhabitants, and in the process the Canaanites had learned to build strong walls about their cities and invent chariots of iron (Judges 1:19). When the Hebrew flood broke across the Jordan River it appeared that the Canaanites were faced with just another episode in the long struggle.

The invaders struck with all the fury of fanatics, but they battled with a stubborn and resourceful foe. In the Old Testament we have two accounts of the campaign which vary considerably in many important details. In Joshua the Hebrews are represented as having won a quick and easy victory and taken almost complete possession of the land. Strange to say, however, many years afterward they are compelled to fight the same battles over again. The more factual and realistic account of the conquest appears in Judges. Here the invaders are portrayed as desert fighters without experience in war or military machinery, battling their way against great odds winning a highland here and a village there until they have established a foothold, with the struggle stretching out through the years.

The Canaanites were not a united people, each locality being responsible for its own defense. The Hebrews were no better organized, having groups of fighters banded together here and there for the purpose of seizing villages and valleys. The result was that the whole land became a melting pot with the forces of the invaders and the defenders inextricably mixed. In the process at least three factors of great significance developed.

10 What were these three factors?

In the first place the Hebrews were unable to reduce the walled cities, but were compelled to leave them standing. Strong fortress-communities like Shechem and Jebus (later renamed Jerusalem) survived through many generations as centers of Canaanite religious, economic, and political influence.

In the second place, the ground was laid for an agelong conflict between the religion of the original Canaanite inhabitants and the Hebrew faith in Yahweh.

In the third place, two diametrically opposed economic philosophies and systems fought it out for the final mastery. There can be no fundamental understanding of many Old Testament situations without a knowledge of this situation.

11 What about the walled cities?

It was in the walled cities that the large landholders congregated. To the cities the rents and profits flowed, and in the cities the government established itself. There, supported by gangs of strong-armed men (*gibborim*, the economic aristocracy of the land was able to maintain itself. These *gibborim* were, actually, hired thugs and ruffians who collected the taxes and sequestered the crops for the benefit of the rich landowners. Much of the significance of their profession has been obscured by the fact that their name, *gibborim*, has usually been translated "men of might" or "mighty men," but from the uses to which they were put it is easy enough to identify their real character.

The cities were at first purely Canaanitish strongholds, but with the advent of David as king of united Israel this changed. That powerful and brilliant monarch, seeing the advantage of a capital situated on a site easily defended, and on the border between the north and south settlements, took over the ancient city of Jebus (II Samuel 5:6-9) together with its large Canaanite population. Now, instead of Jerusalem being a Canaanite center it became a city with a mixed population, many Hebrews becoming the beneficiaries of the economic system in vogue among the Canaanites. In this they were greatly assisted by the policies of David's government.

12 How did David's government assist?

The necessity of presenting a united front against the enemy forced the Hebrews to form a central government; and Saul, a country gentleman, was crowned the first ruler of the little kingdom. His time, for the most part, was given to the management of his estate, and only occasionally periods were given to the organization of the defenses of the realm. The burden of his government rested very lightly upon the backs of the people.

When David came into power the situation changed greatly.

9

The young chieftain began his career with an army of six hundred professional soldiers (*gibborim*—I Samuel 23:13) who lived off the land and the people they "protected." After he became ruler over the nation he put a certain Adoram (or Adoniram) in charge of the "tribute" (II Samuel 20:24); but when we remember that labor was the only form in which taxes could be paid during those early years we discover that this "tribute" was nothing less than forced labor.

David, like all ancient kings, was surrounded by those who took advantage of his friendship to usurp power and special privilege. The king, on the other hand, naturally turned to his friends in the belief that he could depend upon their loyalty. Some of these were his own relatives, while others were members of the "six hundred" who had in one way or another put their leader under obligations to them (II Samuel 8:6; 16:16, 23; 18:2; 19:13; 23:18, 24). The tribute that poured into his coffers from the tariffs collected from the caravans that crossed his borders (I Kings 10:15 describes a similar situation in Solomon's day), and that which was brought back from the conquered provinces, made them all rich and welded the "machine" into a compact organization.

David's reign inaugurated a revolution in the life of the Hebrew people which had results of the most far-reaching significance. Through more than two centuries, for instance, disputes between individuals had been settled in local courts by local judges; but with the establishment of Jerusalem as the capital and the centralization of the government there, David required that all litigants should come to the capital for the trial of their cases. This put the rural districts and rural landowners at a very great disadvantage. During the same two centuries the Hebrews had known little or nothing about taxes. They had rallied to wage war at the call of some rural leader, and when the campaign was over they had returned to their farms. Each man had furnished his own arms, his own food, and his own supplies, with the result that there was no war debt hanging over him when the war was over. But David's standing army and his elaborate court had to be supported, and the only way it could be done was by levying taxes against the farmers. If they could not pay there were obliging moneylenders at the capital, either rich Canaanites or favored members of David's "six hundred," who could be persuaded to make a loan if properly secured. Then, if payment was not forthcoming the security was seized. All this created much discontent and finally resulted in the splitting of the kingdom.

13   How was the kingdom divided?

Solomon, David's successor, was a grand spender. History has glorified him out of all proportion to his true character. Though his reign was unquestionably brilliant, it was also disastrous. So reckless was he in his public expenditures that at one time it became necessary for him to cede twenty cities to one of his creditors in order to meet his obligations (I Kings 9:11). City-born, and reared in the midst of Canaanite influence (II Samuel 5:14; 12:24), Solomon was completely out of touch with the rural Hebrews, his court consisting of a ruthless machine manned by unscrupulous politicians who were supported in power by hired ruffian strong men.

The little kingdom was divided up into twelve districts for purposes of taxation and for the recruiting of forced labor (I Kings 4:7-19), each district being required to furnish one twelfth of the staggering cost of the royal establishment (I Kings 4:22-23). At one time Solomon had 160,000 men rounded up in labor gangs supervised by 3,300 taskmasters (I Kings 5:13-16). During one period in his reign a financial crisis developed in which the nation went off the "silver standard" (I Kings 10:21, 27).

The public-works program included the erection of a gigantic royal palace (I Kings 7:1), a supreme-court building (I Kings 7:2-7; 10:18-20), a palace for his favorite wife (I Kings 7:8; 9:24), and a temple to the honor and for the worship of Yahweh (I Kings 6:1-10, 15-38), much smaller than the rest but yet costing an excessive amount.

All this constituted a burden too great for the poor people and the poorer land to bear, and when the ostentatious monarch died the land was seething with unrest. Consequently, at the very moment that his successor took over the reins of government he found himself face to face with a nation in turmoil. The overseer of forced labor was stoned to death by a mob (I Kings 12:18); the cry of revolt was raised throughout all the north (I Kings 12:16; II Chronicles 10:16); and in a mighty uprising the House of David was repudiated. It was the end of

11

the United Kingdom and the beginning of the two little states of Israel and Judah. Fundamental in the revolt was the question of taxes—the rural landowners and farmers arrayed against the political machine enthroned at Jerusalem, the capital.

14 What about the religious conflict among the Hebrews?

(See Question 10.)

The original inhabitants of the Land of Promise worshiped local gods according to the rituals of the fertility cults. Neighborhood shrines dotted the country over, at each of which pagan ceremonies were conducted that were supposed to persuade the local Baal to grant fertility to the fields and increase to the flocks. Because the idea of increase was uppermost in the theology of the fertility cults, the sex motif was stressed in every imaginable way, and sex practices of various sorts were a conspicuous part of the Baal worship.

With the coming of the Hebrews and their worship of Yahweh a religious conflict immediately appeared. The more brilliant and seductive services at the Baal shrines proved extremely attractive to the rural Hebrews, who found it difficult to explain to themselves why the worship of one more god was to be condemned, especially if there was any chance that it might improve the yield per acre. As a result, the true worshipers of Yahweh were always very much in the minority.

The writer of Kings attempts to lay the responsibility for Israel's tendency toward paganism upon Jeroboam, the first king of Israel, who caused two gilded calves to be erected at popular shrines so that the people would not go down to Jerusalem for their worship and thus continue the political ties with Judah (I Kings 12:25-38). But the charge is not altogether fair. Long before the kingdom split over the question of taxes David had married Canaanite wives (II Samuel 5:13) and extended them considerable latitude in religious matters. Solomon in turn had a populous harem and not only granted his favorites religious liberties but joined with them in worshiping pagan gods, even building altars to pagan divinities inside the sacred precincts of Jerusalem (I Kings 11:1-13).

For at least two hundred years previous to the period we are studying, this conflict between Yahweh and the local Baalim (plural of Baal) had been going on. As early as the middle of the

12

ninth century B.C. two great prophets, Elijah and Elisha, had sensed the issues involved and had struck out fiercely against the economic evils of their times which had come as an accompaniment of the Baal worship. Thereafter for two hundred and seventy-five years the prophets never ceased to demand a complete extermination of Baalism as the nation's only hope of salvation.

15 What about the conflict of economic philosophies?

(See Question 10.)

The Hebrews came in from the desert with the nomad's philosophy of land ownership. A tribe of desert men, wandering over the barren wilderness, believed the range had been given to them by their god, together with its life-producing resources such as oases and wells. Every individual born into the clan was born with certain rights which entitled him to his fair share of all the benefits enjoyed by the clan.

This doctrine of the divine ownership of the land underwent a slight modification when the Hebrews settled in the Land of Promise. When the various families were finally settled on the land that was allotted to them it was with the understanding that their inheritance was never to be sold, but was to be held by the family in perpetuity (Leviticus 25:23, 29-31; Numbers 36:7-8).

To the Baal worshipers, on the other hand, there was no good reason why the land should not be sold if it suited the purposes of its owner to do so. The buying and selling of land had the full approval of their religious tenets. An interesting illustration of the two attitudes is to be found in the readiness with which Araunah, the Canaanite, sold his land to David (II Samuel 24:18-24) and the stubborn refusal of Naboth, the Hebrew, to even trade his little holding to Ahab, the king, though he was offered a good bargain.

With the moneylenders congregated in the cities, and loaning money to hard-pressed farmers that they might pay their taxes, the contest between the cities and the rural districts became a badly mixed affair. As the moneylenders undertook to seize the land in payment of the debts, and employed the *gibborim* commissioned by the courts in ejecting the debtor-landowners, the struggle on the part of the rural farmers against the capitalistic urbanites. As the Assyrian crisis developed, the economic crisis inside Israel and Judah was at its height.

16   What was the Assyrian crisis?

The Assyrian Empire, spreading out across the valleys of the Tigris and Euphrates rivers, was a very ancient state. Its history ran back into the dim and misty centuries to a time when written records were only beginning to take form. At one time Assyrian armies had penetrated deep into the region of the Nile, but for several hundred years prior to the eighth century B.C. the Empire had been altogether occupied with enemies on its eastern and northern borders, or with internal problems. Meanwhile the Palestinian world, with its dozen or more little states, had been allowed to live in peace.

In 746 B.C. an energetic and ambitious monarch came to the Assyrian throne in the person of Tiglath Pileser III, sometimes called "the Roman of the East." Under his vigorous leadership the nation's affairs were quickly put in order and Assyria began to dream again of world conquest, which meant the subjugation of Egypt.

17   What was the state of affairs in Egypt?

Egypt was a shoestring strip of a country clinging to the banks of the Nile and content to live in the luxury made possible by the incredibly rich soil of the valley. Cut off from the rest of the world by sand and desert, Egypt had been content for the most part to develop her own culture and amass her own wealth in comparative isolation and safety. On a few occasions ambitious Pharaohs (such as Amenhotep and Thutmose in the sixteenth century) struck out toward the east with considerable success. But by the time our story begins Egypt was living quietly behind her own borders threatening no one. Assyria was the aggressor.

18   What was the cause of Assyria's aggression?

The territory of Assyria, lying along the uplands of the Tigris and Euphrates, was a stern and reluctant land which yielded its fruit only at a price. It supported its people adequately but at the cost of much hard labor. This of course contributed to the nation's strength but not to its spirit of content. The rich, lush valleys of the Nile and of the lower levels of the Tigris and

Euphrates were a constant temptation, and the vast stores of loot which might be seized by a successful campaign stirred the cupidity of emperor and people alike.

Equally important were the political ambitions of Tiglath Pileser III, who came to the throne as the successor of a long line of incompetents infatuated with the dream of becoming master of the world. Having consolidated his position inside his Empire, and having built up a huge war machine in doing so, he faced what was, to him, a pleasant necessity—a new war front. Under such circumstances Egypt was the inevitable choice. Thus the first great world crisis was precipitated.

19 Why call it a world crisis?

Until the beginning of the eighth century B.C. the world of the East was divided up into a large number of small states—tiny kingdoms which were usually content to live inside their own borders and attend to their own affairs. None were of any great military or political significance. Their armies were little more than bands of raiders intent on pilage. Professional soldiers were almost unknown. It was still the early morning of civilization, and political ambitions had not yet had time to develop in terms of world domination.

When Assyria struck at Egypt it was something new in world politics. True, there had been other times when invading armies had ravaged over wide areas, but Tiglath Pileser III aimed at one great political organization which should rule the world. Huge armies had to be transported great distances. Numerous kingdoms and peoples were involved. The fortunes of every little state in the ancient world were affected by the outcome. Neutrality was almost an impossibility, and independence degenerated into a mirage. In such a world diplomacy and intrigue came into their own.

20 How did the crisis affect Israel?

Israel was the northern Hebrew Kingdom and would be the first to feel the blow as the Assyrian armies came marching south, en route to Egypt. There was no highway by which Tiglath Pileser could reach the Nile without crossing Israel's borders. Neutrality was out of the question. Her land was certain to be a battleground. She was compelled to choose her role—either as an enemy of Assyria and an ally of Egypt, or as an enemy of Egypt and an ally of Assyria. In either case an alliance meant vassalage.

21 How did the crisis affect Judah?

Judah's position was slightly better. Her territory did not extend as far west as the sea, but lay east of the great trade routes, atop the Judean hills. Jerusalem, her capital, was difficult of access and located somewhat off the beaten path. It was possible for armies of Assyria to march down to Egypt and ignore Judah without striking a blow. Furthermore, the territory of Judah could scarcely have tempted any conqueror of great pride, for it offered little reward for any extensive campaign. It contained no mineral wealth, no great forests, no broad and fertile plains, and no stores of precious stones. It was barren, sterile, rugged, and yielded its livings grudgingly. The geographical differences between the two little Hebrew kingdoms produced marked differences in their political policies.

22 What was the policy of Israel?

All Israel looked upon Assyria as an inescapable adversary. There was then but one party—the war party. Her problem was to find allies who would stand with her against Assyria.

23 What was the policy of Judah?

The southern kingdom, because of its more advantageous location, had a choice between several policies, and as a consequence there were at least three political parties. Some insisted that Judah should enter into an alliance with the other Palestinian nations, aided by Egypt. Others believed her one hope lay in becoming an ally of Assyria, which of course involved the payment of a huge annual tribute for "protection." But a small group, of whom Isaiah became the leader, counseled a policy of isolation.

24 What was the Egyptian policy?

Egypt was the archconspirator and meddler of the ancient world. Her chief interest naturally was in protecting her own borders, and this meant a narrow isthmus of sand which connected Africa and Asia—the same isthmus alongside of which the Hebrews had lived during the days of their Egyptian bondage. Across this isthmus all the trade routes passed, crowded with caravans and traders from every point in Asia.

Between Egypt and Assyria there lay a considerable number of small city-states and at least three rather sizable kingdoms—Judah, Israel, and Syria. Before Egypt could be invaded these would have to be subdued. It was logical then that Pharaoh would make every possible effort to persuade the Palestinian states to resist Assyria with all their might.

Whatever Egypt lacked in military skill she made up for in diplomacy, and her emissaries went everywhere making glib promises. Whenever a small nation was found wavering, these diplomats poured out assurances of aid, great rewards, and great privilege in "the new order" which would follow Assyria's defeat. In times of crisis when capitals were in peril and when foes were within striking distance, this help did not arrive; and one of the Hebrew prophets who took the long view of history characterized her very aptly when he said, "Pharaoh . . . is but a noise" (Jeremiah 46:17).

25 What was the Assyrian policy?

The mighty Empire had but one purpose in her program; she warred for plunder. She spread no culture, built no cities, encouraged no civilization, and established no social order better than slavery. She rode upon the back of the world like some gigantic leech, sucking the lifeblood of every people she conquered, utterly ruthless, altogether cruel, barbaric without apology, warring without cause, and plundering without mercy. When she conquered a nation it was as if some black night of hopelessness had settled down upon the people. For two hundred years her very name and that of her capital, Nineveh, were synonyms for terror throughout the East.

26 What was the policy of Syria?

Lying just north of Israel, and nearest to the mighty Assyrian Empire, was the little kingdom of Syria (the student must never confuse it with Assyria). Its capital, Damascus, was a proud metropolis, well fortified, rich, and a tempting prize for any conqueror. As one of the most glamorous cities of the ancient East, if often gave its name to the Kingdom; and many biblical writers speak of Damascus when they mean Syria.

This nation had gone through a varied experience during the centuries, slipping in and out of vassalage many times. At one time, not so long before the opening of our story, both Judah and Israel had paid tribute to Syria; but in 750 B.C. the three kingdoms were all practically independent. One thing was certain, however: whenever Assyria chose to launch her campaign Syria was plainly marked as the first victim because of her geographical location.

27 What preparation had they made for the crisis?

Syria had long sensed the danger and had made considerable efforts to gird herself for the struggle. She knew full well the might of the enemy and sought allies with desperate eagerness.

Israel, potentially, was strongest, but her leaders were ignorant of the trends in world politics and could not think in anything more than provincial terms. Almost half a century of exaggerated prosperity had sapped her strength and made her incapable of realizing the true state of world affairs. Perhaps she should not be judged too harshly, for the factors and trends of the time were something new in human experience. Never before had she been compelled to deal with a foe that was bent on world domination. Heretofore she had been engaged with small nations that were content with predatory raids and minor conquests.

Judah was brave but incompetently led. Her king, at the height of the crisis, was weak, inexperienced, and young. Her nobles were debauched; her people were unaware of the seriousness of the situation; and her isolation persuaded her that she was impregnable. The one saving element in the situation in this little kingdom was the foresight, courage, leadership, and vision of two brilliant and militant prophets—Micah and Isaiah.

The most dangerous aspect of the situation was the softening process that had gone on inside the nations through a period of nearly fifty years.

28 What was this softening process?

During the first half of the eighth century B.C. Assyria had been preoccupied with border troubles in the north and east.

These had diverted her attention and given the Palestinian states a breathing spell. Comparative peace had prevailed for something like forty years (790 to 750 B.C.). With peace came commerce, and almost half a century of profitable trade had seen changes take place which affected almost every aspect of the nations' lives. In the case of the Hebrew kingdoms money flowed in upon them in a veritable tide. As a result, life in both nations underwent a radical transformation. And even in this commerce which produced so much wealth there was a certain sinister significance.

29 What about the wealth that flowed through Palestine?

Assyria, engaged in war, used up her labor force and was in need of grain with which to feed her population. Grain, being one of the principal exports of Egypt, was imported into Assyria to supplement her own crops. There is a sense in which it is true that Egypt and the Palestinian states helped Assyria by furnishing the materials upon which she fed, just as the United States and Great Britain furnished the oil and other war supplies by which Japan made war on them in 1941.

30 What produced the sudden prosperity in Palestine?

Aside from the fact that any time of peace sees goods accumulate, an economic condition contributed very largely to the prosperity of the Palestinian states. According to the ancient law any king was at liberty to assess customs duties against any merchandise carried across his borders. These duties might be paid either in cash or in merchandise. If the duties were paid in goods, then the goods had to be consumed or sold. If consumed they raised the standard of living for the people of the land; if sold they stimulated trade. Forty years of peace which made the highways of the world safe for caravans of merchandise had seen a revival of trade all through Palestine, with Israel and Judah prospering in a very large way, and Syria only a little less so.

31 Why were Israel and Judah special beneficiaries?

Every great trade route between Asia and Africa stretched down across Palestine. All passed through the territory of

Israel, for there was no way of reaching Egypt without crossing her borders. Such caravans as ventured across the Arabian Desert came through Judah, en route to Egypt. Thus the two little kingdoms constituted a bottleneck through which the traffic of the world poured. They were in a position to collect taxes from the entire East; and they did so, with the result that a social revolution was going on inside their own lives.

32 What was this social revolution?

It was a transformation of the life of the people which appeared in at least ten different aspects. The total result was so significant that not one phase of life was left untouched.

33 What was the first great change?

The nations passed from an agricultural to a commercial life. Individuals who lived near to the trade routes found it highly profitable to buy from one caravan and sell to another. Then there were always supplies to be sold to the travelers. Tourists and traders usually leave money behind; and just as eating houses and filling stations line the modern highway, so markets and bazaars sprang up along the ancient roads. Families that had depended upon the land now began to live off the traders and travelers. In many instances those who lived at some distance from the trade routes sold out and moved in closer to the trading centers. Commerce began to displace agriculture in the life of the nation.

34 What was the second change?

Large cities began to grow up. Until the time of which we speak there had been few large cities in the Hebrew kingdoms. In most instances there had been only ancient Canaanite cities with a large percentage of "alien population." But with the rising tide of commerce the Hebrew farmers began drifting into the cities, some out of choice and some driven by necessity. For the first time a landless class of considerable proportions appeared—people who depended upon their day's labor for subsistence. This migration was attended by overcrowding, unemployment periods, exploitation of workers, abandoned farms, and various other social changes.

35   What was the third change?

The development of an economic aristocracy. As usually happens, the new wealth which arose from commerce flowed into the pockets of those already well to do. Government favorites secured the jobs as tax collectors and kept a liberal share as payment for their labors. The royal establishments, aping the gaudy and glamorous courts of neighboring kingdoms, piled up the tax load. Farmers who were unable to pay their taxes borrowed from the rich money lords in the cities, giving their land as security. Foreclosures which collected the loans drove the farmers to the cities or resulted in absentee landlordism. The very rich and the very poor lived behind the same city walls. Here and there some recalcitrant farmer resisted the tide, and the courts were enlisted, with their *gibborim*, to help the moneylenders work their will.

36   What was the fourth change?

The first appearance of a working class. For five months out of the year commerce on the Mediterranean was impractical on account of storms. This meant that all the normal trade between Africa and the lands to the north had to cross Israel and pay tribute to the Hebrew kings. In the busy season there was a lively demand for workers, but in the slack season they were idle. All the modern problems of unemployment appeared with the exception of the fact that the workers were not organized. No one came to the defense of the poor, for no national conscience had developed as yet on the subject of social justice.

37   What was the fifth great change?

The appearance of a class of defenseless poor. When the Hebrews came out of the desert there were no rich and no poor among them. If any tribe had food all members of the tribe had food. If any were poor all were poor. But once they were settled upon the land each man's fortune depended upon his own industry and skill. Some were good farmers and some were not. So long as a man owned the land he had an element of security. But when land began to be sold a landless class arose, and this in turn became a poor class. In the time we are studying no man made the cause of the poor his responsibility. This was a later

21

development which came as a result of the activities of the prophets who spoke in the name of Jehovah.

38 What was the sixth change?

The problem of urbanization. As cities grew up all the problems of slums, congestion, disorganization of home life, disparities in social status, extravagances, short weights and balances, ostentation and poverty appeared. Life became fashionable and superficial.

39 What was the seventh great change?

The problem of highly concentrated wealth. When the first trickle of trade appeared the nobles and aristocrats were on hand to collect the customs. Wealth flowed into the pockets of those already rich. Callousness and cruelty developed, and all over the land the poor suffered such woes as they had never known before. Ancestral holdings were appropriated by the money-lenders, and many of the fine old virtues of the nation disappeared. All the time the kingdoms deluded themselves into thinking they were enjoying unprecedented prosperity.

40 What was the eighth change?

The government itself was corrupted. The rich nobles found it very convenient to ignore the ancient *mishpat* which the people had brought in with them from the desert and from the teachings of Moses. The primitive laws of the Hebrews were designed to provide justice for the humblest man of the nation. This simple system, based on the idea of the sanctity of the individual and resting back on the authority of Yahweh (the Hebrews called it *mishpat*), distinguished Israel and Judah from all the other ancient states. It was the undermining of this concept of justice which constituted the most serious damage being done. The whole governmental system, including the courts, was in process of being thoroughly corrupted; and inside the capitals (Jerusalem in Judah and Samaria in Israel) a ring of "Tammany politicians" came into existence, composed of rich landowners and capitalists. These dominated the government and manipulated it to their own benefit.

41 What was the ninth change?

The rising tide of immorality. The beneficiaries of the new economic system, unprepared for the moral hazards it entailed, turned to dissipation. The liquor trade flourished, morals deteriorated, and the sturdy old peasant character of the people began to break down in high places. Nothing more serious could have happened than this corruption of the nations' leadership just at the time when two kingdoms faced the greatest crisis of their career.

42 What was the tenth great change?

The worship of Yahweh was corrupted. When the Hebrews came into the Promised Land from the desert they had only forty years' experience in the worship of Yahweh, or Jehovah. In the Land of Promise they came in contact with a people who had worshiped their Baalim for centuries, and down through the years the conflict between the religion of Yahweh and the religion of Baal was one of the major matters of the race's life. Hebrew prophets were united in their opposition to paganism.

In the eighth century B.C. this conflict took a new turn. The Hebrews were doing business with men from the ends of the earth, and many strange gods came in the caravans with the strange goods. New altars began to appear in Hebrew cities, at which strange rites were practiced. The merchant has always found it to his advantage to be tolerant of rival religious faiths for the sake of sales, and the Hebrews of the little kingdoms found it was good business to assume a broad-minded attitude. Pagan ceremonies were taken over bodily, in some instances, and became a part of the worship of Jehovah.

As an accompaniment of the paganizing process it is easy to trace a social process by which the destinies of the people fell into the keeping of exploiters and moneylenders. Life was all of one piece—as the worship of Yahweh was diluted the ancient *mishpat* was imperiled.

43 Were the nations aware of these changes?

That was the tragedy: the leaders (usually the beneficiaries of the new system) thought it was good because it was good for them, and none seemed to be conscious of the seriousness of the social changes taking place inside the nations. Of all those who had any part in fashioning national policies only the prophets seemed to be aware of the meaning of deep, underlying issues.

44 What part did the prophets play in the crisis?

Each of the four prophets we are to study was immersed in the life of which he was a part. Not one of them was a dreamer, with his eyes fixed on some far-off divine event. Each had made a study of his times—of the political forces at work, and of the moral issues involved—and each was perfectly sure he knew the secret by which the nations' security might be insured. Each believed profoundly that he was speaking the mind of Yahweh when he preached to one of the nations. Each was amazingly well informed on the subject of world conditions, and the message of each was directed at the nations and dealt with the crisis through which Israel and Judah were passing. None of them organized any "pressure group" and none held any political office, but each depended upon the power of preaching to correct the wrongs against which he inveighed. They were, in the best sense of the word, preachers of the gospel of Yahweh, and yet they were all laymen. There was not one professional religionist among them.

45 Were they political prophets?

They were men to whom all of life seemed sacred, to be lived under the eye and subject to the approval of God. They did not divide life into two compartments—sacred and secular. It was all of one piece and must be made satisfactory to God in every aspect. This was their fundamental message. Social standards, economic systems, religious rites, political rights, national policies, sacrifices, personal morals—all had to have the approval of God. It is highly significant that none of them dealt with the question of "personal religion."

46 Why did they not deal with personal religion?

Because religion to them was a national or racial matter and not an individual question. A careful study of Amos, Hosea, Isaiah, and Micah reveals the fact that their messages were always delivered to the nation, or to individuals as members of the nation. They were concerned with saving the nation, content in the belief that the individual would be saved if the nation were saved. The sins of individuals and classes were always viewed as part of the national sinning, and individuals were rebuked for their sins not as individuals but as segments of

24

the nation. What we think of as "personal religion" did not develop among the Hebrews until a hundred and fifty years later, under the teachings of Jeremiah.

47 Were they professional prophets?

Each of the eighth-century prophets was an individualist who had no connections with any professionally religious group. At least one of them (Amos) proudly disclaimed all connections with the professional prophets (7:14).

48 What does this mean?

Among the Hebrews there were those who were known as "sons of the prophets." By this it was not understood that they were physical descendants of prophets, but that they were members of a professionally prophetic group. They were, in a sense, fortunetellers; and the public believed they spoke for God and that they received their messages while in some ecstatic state (I Kings 11:25; II Kings 3:15; Ezekiel 1:3; 3:14; 8:1; 33:22; 37:1). At times, because of their emotional excitement, they were thought to be demented (Jeremiah 29:26). They made their living by their profession (I Samuel 9:7-8), and their custom of prophesying for pay had brought them into no small disrepute.

Between these professional prophets and the "true prophets" whose writings we find in the Old Testament, there was almost constant friction. It is highly important that the student keep in mind at all times the difference between the professional prophets and the true prophets who produced so large a portion of our Old Testament.

49 Who was Amos?

He was a poor man, without social importance, who earned a precarious living among the limestone hills southeast of Jerusalem, herding sheep (1:1; 7:14) and gathering wild figs in the lowlands which he prepared for the market as food for the very poor. He was, in every sense, a son of the people, and it is of very great significance that such a man should write the first complete book of the Bible. It is for this reason that the student should know something about his background.

50 What about Amos' background?

The fact that his father's name is not mentioned indicates that he did not belong to one of the landed families. Those who belonged to honorable lines were usually careful to identify themselves by their family names.

Amos was a man without prestige, political importance, wealth, schooling, or priestly connection. The sheep he tended were a peculiar breed whose wool was of the finest quality. The housewives of the region of Tekoa enjoyed a wide reputation for their homespun because of the superior quality of the wool they used (Proverbs 31:24). The shepherds themselves were the butt of much ridicule because of the bizarre appearance of the sheep they tended, which were almost naked of wood about the head and face.

The figs they gathered were from the semiwild sycamore, which grew in the lowlands east of Tekoa. They became fit for eating only after they had been bruised during the ripening process. The shepherd was under the necessity of climbing the trees during the ripening season and pinching them so that they might become a sticky sweet mass suitable for eating. These two occupations will give an indication of Amos' lowly station in life.

51 When did Amos write his book?

We are fortunate in being able to fix an approximate date. In the very first verse of his book Amos names the two reigning kings of Israel and Judah, and in addition he mentions an earthquake. From these, and from other references, scholars are agreed that it must have been very near to the year 750 B.C. when amos wrote his message down.

52 To whom did Amos preach?

Although he was a Judean, he did his preaching in the kingdom of Israel. As a matter of fact, Judah was something of a vassal to Israel at the moment, and there is a sense in which it can be said that he was a citizen of both kingdoms. But as a Judean he was held in contempt by the ruling class of Israel (7:12-13).

53 What were the conditions of the times?

Amos preached in the midst of a postwar boom. About the beginning of the eighth century B.C. Israel's fortunes had been at their lowest ebb (II Kings 13:7). Overpowered by Syria in the north she had been stripped of almost all her possessions; but Assyrian pressure on Syria saved the day, and the latter part of Jeroboam's reign found the little kingdom (750 B.C.) enjoying unprecedented prosperity (II Kings 13:5). Her borders had been restored; her domestic life had been made orderly; and the confidence of the people in themselves was restored (II Kings 14:25-27). Everyone was optimistic, and life seemed highly satisfactory. Trade was good, and money flowed freely. No one sensed the impending danger.

54 What was the impending danger?

Assyrian forces were gathering for the attack on Egypt. The armies had been trained in the hard campaigns against the Haldians in the north; war materials were being assembled in vast quantities; the nation's domestic affairs were being put in order in anticipation of the greatest test of strength in all her history. Much of this, of course, was going on secretly; but enough of the facts were known to warn discerning leaders of trouble to come. Not so in Israel and probably no more so in Judah.

55 Was Amos aware of the situation?

He probably was. He predicted trouble for Israel, though he never named the troublemaker (2:6; 3:11-12, 14; 5:1, 27). That would hardly have been necessary, for there was no other nation in the world at the time which Israel had any reason to fear.

56 Why did Amos turn to preaching?

One of the most interesting things about his ministry was his stout denial of any professional prophetic connections (7:14-15). He seemed to sense the fact that the professional prophets were in bad odor and he disclaimed all relations with them. But at the same time he believed that he was called of God to speak to the nation, and was very positive in declaring that his message was divinely given (3:8; 7:1, 8, 15; 8:1; 9:1). He had a series of visions

27

which left him with the conviction that he must speak.

57 What about those visions?

There were five in all: (1) the invasion of locusts (7:1-3); (2) the drought (7:4-6); (3) the plumbline (7:7-9); (4) the basket of fruit (8:1-3); (5) the stricken pillar (9:1-4).

Amos tells about them in forthright fashion; but we cannot be sure whether they were special experiences from which the prophet derived meanings or psychic experiences which he interpreted. At any rate it makes little difference. The important thing is that as a result of them Amos became profoundly convinced that he was divinely called to speak (7:15).

58 What training had he had for such a career?

There was little in his training as a shepherd which fitted him for service as a prophet. The sternness of the desert was in his blood and became a characteristic of his speech. Necessity sharpened his wits, and the solitude of the wilderness gave him ample time to think his way through on the problems of his time. His occasional trips to the markets in the north provided him with the facts and material upon which to meditate. The total result was that this humble shepherd came out of the wilderness of Tekoa a man on fire for God and justice.

59 Where is Tekoa?

It was a name applied to an area south, and a little east, of Jerusalem. Nothing remains today of any villages or settlements, and the best we can do is to identify the region. But having done that we have a clue to Amos' ministry.

60 What is the clue?

Among the hills of Judah life went on very much as it had in the wilderness. Just across the Jordan, on the east, lay the broad wastes of the Arabian Desert; and the inhabitants of the region of Tekoa were only a few miles removed from the hard, barren, exacting life of nomads. Among them the principles of the desert *mishpat* still prevailed, and to such a prophet as Amos the "modern ways" of the new commercial centers of Judah and Israel were indicative of a general dissolution of life. We must never forget this desert background as we listen to him preach.

61 Where did Amos begin preaching?

Most of the prophet's simple needs could be satisfied in the desert, but he was under the necessity of going to the northern and southern markets with wool and figs to exchange for those goods which the desert did not supply. Those trips took him to the Judean markets of Hebron, Jerusalem and Beersheba; but they also took him to the larger and better markets of Gilgal, Bethel, and Samaria in Israel. He may even have traveled as far as Damascus in Syria; but from his book we know that the one fateful experience which started him off as a writing prophet occurred at the shrine of Bethel.

62 What was that fateful experience?

Having gone to Bethel for business reasons and having visited the shrine whereat he proposed to worship Yahweh, he had been profoundly moved by the evils he found in the city and the utter indifference of the religious leaders. Seizing an opportune time during the festivities at the shrine, he had taken his position on the steps near to the altar and delivered a speech to the worshipers in which he lashed out at the iniquities of the day, not even sparing the royal court.

The religious festivals at Bethel were accompanied by much wine-drinking and other excesses, and the picture of this stern desert prophet in vigorous denunciation of the half-drunken throng is one of the most stirring scenes in the Old Testament.

Amaziah, the priest in charge of the shrine, expelled him because of his reference to the royal house, charging him with treason and driving him from the city. As a result of this experience he wrote down the gist of his message, together with an abbreviated account of his experience, and this written record is what we have in the Old Testament.

63 Did he do all his preaching in Bethel?

So far as we know, he did. Some scholars think he may have made several speeches and that his book contains the summary, but there is nothing to prove such a theory.

64 Do we have any other information about Amos?

Strange to say, there is no mention of the prophet elsewhere in the Old Testament. In the nine short chapters of his book we have all the information about him that the Scriptures give.

65 Did Amos understand his times?

As a shepherd deep in the hills of Judah, far removed from the busy life of the cities, and remote from the changing civilization of the kingdom which was brought about by the rising tide of commercialism, he was in a position to get a perspective on life which those who lived in the midst of feverish activity were almost sure to miss. On his trips to the markets he traveled the crowded caravan routes and listened to the gossip of the world. In the trading centers he found men who could give him news from everywhere. His sharp eyes penetrated the gilded disguises of the new culture and saw suffering and wretchedness festering just under the surface. His book bears evidence of having been written by a close observer, a keen analyst, a careful thinker, and a man with an exalted sense of honor and justice. Above all, he was a man with an acute sense of God.

66 What weakness did he see?

1. He was sure that Israel had lost favor with Yahweh because injustices were allowed to go unrebuked and uncorrected.
2. He sensed some impending disaster and was convinced that Israel was utterly unprepared to stand up against it.
3. He saw that the strength of the nation was corroded away by its injustices and immoralities.
4. He believed that the false confidence which lulled the nation into a fatuous complacency was due to a popular religious doctrine generally called the "Day of Jehovah."
5. To Amos it was plain that the ill-founded optimism of the nation was a by-product of its false conceptions of God.

67 How had Israel lost the favor of Yahweh?

According to Hebrew belief the covenant of Sinai established a special partnership between Yahweh and the Hebrew nations. If the people kept the laws of Yahweh, Yahweh was bound to protect them. It was of the utmost importance, then, that there should be a perfectly clear understanding of these laws.

The established priests taught Israel that the one sure way to

30

keep the good will of Yahweh was to offer sacrifices on altars according to the correct form, and to perform certain ceremonies in an acceptable fashion. Having performed those rites and ceremonies correctly, they believed Yahweh was under obligations to protect them against all foes. They had no thought that personal morals or social behavior had anything to do with the matter. And the fact that Jeroboam's reign had been attended by a brilliant prosperity seemed to add sanction to the priests' theory.

Amos, on the other hand, with his ideals of desert *mishpat*, believed that Yahweh was interested in moral behavior and social justice. To an orthodox Hebrew a person who did not offer sacrifices in the correct fashion was a traitor, but to Amos one who worked injustices on neighbors was a traitor. To him social immorality, not neglected altars, was high treason (2:6-8).

68 What about the impending disaster?

It could hardly have been possible for Amos to travel the highways of his day without hearing reports of Assyria's military preparations. News of the Empire's plans was common gossip, and all the East was agog with rumors. But Amos never mentions Assyria by name. The nearest he comes to identifying Israel's foe is his reference to the captivity that is coming from "beyond Damascus" (5:27). But of the ultimate fate of the nation he had no doubt. It was to be destroyed (4:2-3), and nothing more than a tattered and bloody fragment would be left (3:12). It was to be forsaken and prostrate (5:2), with its population decimated (5:3).

69 What about the "Day of Jehovah"?

The religious leaders of the nation had taught the people that they were the chosen of Yahweh and that there was a day coming when all the enemies of Israel and Judah would be destroyed and the little Hebrew kingdoms would be exalted. Careful performances of the shrine ceremonies and liberal sacrifices at the altars would hasten the coming of that day. In a rather curious fashion the doctrine resembled the modern doctrine of "the second coming of Jesus," as that creed is held by some people.

But Amos saw the "Day of Jehovah" as something entirely

different. True, he believed in such a day, but instead of it being a day of triumph and vindication it was to be a day of judgment and retribution—a day so terrible that it would be like a man who, fleeing from a lion, is met by a bear, or like one who leans against a wall in exhaustion only to be bitten by a scorpion (5:18-20)—a day to be dreaded, not one to be anticipated.

70 Why did Amos condemn the optimism of the people?

Because it blinded them to the terrible perils with which they were confronted. Indeed, Amos believed that the excessive emphasis placed upon rite and ceremony was a part of the nation's undoing. There is a sense in which he would have agreed with the Russian Communists who say, "Religion is the opiate of the people."

Let there be no mistake about the matter: there was a very great deal of religion in Amos' day, but it was an ill-founded faith (5:4-6). It trusted in the sacrifices and ceremonies at the very moment that Amos saw the nation perishing for lack of moral character and social conscience. He could see terrible suffering ahead (9:2-4), from which ceremonies and sacrifices could not possibly save them (3:11; 4:4-5; 6:8, 14).

Underneath the shallow optimism of the people Amos saw four great cancers eating away at the vitals of the nation so serious that they threatened the very existence of the Hebrew kingdom.

71 What was the first?

The ancient land system of the nation was breaking up. The desert *mishpat* was being repudiated by the government in favor of the unmoral system of the surrounding paganism. Land was being bought and sold and ancient families of substance were losing their inheritance. It was an economic upheaval of major proportions.

72 What was the second?

When the Hebrews came out of the desert they were probably the most chaste nation in the world so far as sex matters were concerned. Although polygamy was practiced among them, prostitution in any commercial sense was practically unknown.

But contact with the pagan religions of the Canaanites had been making heavy inroads on these standards. All those religions were organized about the sex motif or principle of increase, and prostitution at the shrines was a part of the religious worship of the people. As commerce invaded the Hebrew kingdoms, the pagan religions set up altars in the cities and made a frank appeal to the sensuality of the public. The moral standards of the Hebrews, far in advance of their neighbors, suffered greatly as a consequence.

In the desert, when the people wandered from one oasis to another, it was seldom possible for a tribe to stop long enough to grow vines that would produce grapes for wine; but among the Canaanites drunkenness was common, and the Hebrews took to the habit under the tutelage of their pagan neighbors. By Amos' day religious feasts had become drunken orgies. The riches of the nobility, a product of the new commercialism, increased the temptation to drunkenness, and the leaders of Israel were fast becoming sodden and dissolute. The general immorality of the day was pronounced among the aristocrats because they had the money to spend on dissipation, and their example popularized it for all the people. The religion of the day imposed no restrictions, the total result being a breakdown of character all along the line.

73 What was the third?

With the coming of the traders came strange gods. It soon became the fashion for many altars to pagan gods to be erected in Hebrew towns and cities. Various cults throve alongside one another. Many practices were taken over from the strange gods and made a part of the worship of Yahweh, including the "sacred prostitution." It was not that the theology of the Hebrews was affected, but their whole philosophy of life. The ancient Yahweh worship, with its insistence upon *mishpat* or desert justice, was undermined by the prevailing paganism. As the cities dominated the rural districts the land became inundated by idolatry, which was always accompanied by economic oppression. In all this the poor were the greatest sufferers, for they had everything to lose if the religion of Yahweh went into decline. It was for this reason that Amos defended the cause of Yahweh; he knew that he and his would lose their all if the ancient faith collapsed.

74 What was the fourth?

When the Hebrews came out of the desert the spirit of individualism was strong among them. The humblest and poorest had rights which the richest and strongest were bound to protect. Men were not judged by the class to which they belonged, nor were they granted privileges on any such basis. A Hebrew was a Hebrew because of the blood that ran in his veins. But with the development of the new civilization, and with the coming of the new money economy, men came to be judged by what they owned rather than by what they were. Society began splitting up into classes, the denominator being economic, and against all this Amos cried out with all his might.

75 Were matters worse in Israel than in Judah?

In some respects. In the first place, more than a score of old Canaanite cities had survived the Hebrew invasion of the Land of Promise. Although they were situated along the borders of ancient Israel, their influence spread across the land, and the rich landowners who made their homes therein became very powerful as a result of the new prosperity. This constituted a social and economic force of very great importance.

In the second place, Israel was a nation that bestrode the great trade routes and was more deeply involved in the commercialism of the times. Jerusalem was a country capital somewhat removed from the main current of affairs, while Samaria was a busy metropolis in the very center of the scene. Though the same social forces were at work in both kingdoms, the effects were more noticeable in Israel. But to understand the book of Amos we must look at Israel through the shepherd's eyes.

76 How was life different for Amos?

He was a countryman to whom every living thing was infinitely precious. When he saw the rich grandees of Bethel eating little day-old lambs and wobbly calves (6:4) in their extravagance, it seemed to him utterly sinful, callous, and

34

reprobate. In the desert where he tended sheep everyone was poor; and the luxurious houses and expensive furnishings of the cities outraged his sense of justice, especially when he knew the processes by which they were obtained. He was indignant when the rich were complacent in the midst of the sufferings of the poor. There was a certain rough-and-ready justice in the desert, but in the cities he found the courts corrupt and judges accepting bribes openly (5:12). In the desert men defended one another, but in the cities they preyed upon one another.

Amos was a poor man, but his poverty was the product of narrow valleys, sterile soil, and a hard country in which to make a living. The poverty of Israel was the result of oppression, exploitation, injustice, and corruption. All Israel might have lived in reasonable plenty if the land had been justly ruled and well administered. It was against the injustices which caused the poverty that Amos inveighed.

77 Did not the government protect the people?

The rich, the powerful, and the nobility—these were the government, with the judges of the courts a part of the vicious system (5:7-11), all protected by laws dictated by the money lords. This was what aroused Amos' ire. No one had the moral judgment to see, or the courage to protest against, the social injustices that were making life hideous for the masses of the people. Short weights, faulty balances (8:5), and kindred evils went unrebuked. So anxious were the big businessmen to make money that they chafed under the small restraints imposed by the feast days, restless for the dawn of a business day when they could plunge again into the mad melee of money-making (8:4-6).

78 Did not the priests protest?

Organized religion had no social conscience. Its sole concern was ritual and ceremony. Priests felt no more responsible for social wrongs than modern preachers feel for technical errors of engineers. Such matters were esteemed to be entirely outside the realm of religious thought.

79 Was the nation irreligious?

Not at all. In fact, it was very religious. Its shrines were

35

crowded, its services elaborate, its sacrifices expensive, its devotions meticulous, the sabbaths properly observed, and the feasts numerous (5:21-23). *But it was a religion that did not care about the poor.*

80 What did Amos call sinful?

In contrast to the priests who said that failure to sacrifice rams and bullocks was a sin, Amos demanded just dealings and fair treatment of one's fellows. No priest ever considered the possibility of shutting a man away from the privileges of the shrines because he heaped injustices upon the weak or robbed the poor. An Israelite at Bethel might have done these things and suffer no rebuke or embarrassment.

Not so with Amos. The sins he condemned were not ceremonial failures nor were they ritualistic oversights. They were acts and attitudes which are considered sins today by all right-minded persons, but which in Amos' day no one considered sinful. That is an indication of the distance the race has traveled since the eighth century B.C. Graft, bribery, prostitution, cruelty, drunkenness, embezzlement, corruption of courts, the defeat of justice—none of these terrible evils were associated with religion in any way in the thinking of the priests or the people.

81 Where did Amos preach his sermon?

At a city called Bethel, near to the southern border of Israel. Here was the favorite shrine of the reigning monarch, Jeroboam II; and anyone speaking there was speaking to the government (7:12).

82 Who was in charge of the shrine?

The original order of the priests established by David was in Jerusalem, of course. But Jeroboam I, who founded the shrine as a center of Hebrew worship following the division of the kingdom, had created a priestly order of his own (I Kings 12:31); and in 750 B.C. the priest in charge of the shrine was an appointee of the government—a man named Amaziah (7:10). He owed his position to the king's favor (7:13) and was naturally interested in defending the royal prerogatives. The shrine, on the other hand, was supported in large part out of the royal treasury, and the priests who ministered there were under deep obligations to the king and nobles who worshiped there. It was a perfect instance of the state owning the church.

83 How did Amos proceed?

For all our information at this point we must depend upon the book of Amos, but it is comparatively easy to reconstruct the scene. The prophet took his place at some point of vantage and at an opportune moment began to address the crowd. He opened with an indictment against Israel's neighbors—nations whose cruelties and outrages were matters of common knowledge throughout the east. Damascus, Gaza, Ashdod, Tyre, Edom, Ammon, Moab, and even Judah came in for a vigorous condemnation. By this adroit approach (1:1—2:5)—for us a graphic picture of a cruel world—the prophet won the sympathy and attention of his crowd.

84 To what did the prophet refer?

The various nations had been guilty of terrible outrages against their neighbors. It was true of all the world that there was neither justice nor mercy abroad anywhere in the land. Syria—whom he calls Damascus—had treated Israel brutally for more than a hundred years. Gaza, one of the Philistine cities near the Egyptian border, was the center of the slave trade (1:6-7), recruiting its stock of slaves by raiding villages of southern Judah. Moab had defiled the bodies of its dead enemies (2:1), which was about the worse crime possible according to the opinion of the day. The Ammonites had violated all decency in their cruelties (1:13-15). In thus charging the nations with sin in the name of Yahweh, Amos took a long step forward in religious thinking.

85 What was Amos' forward step?

Among all the people of the ancient world it was believed that each nation had a god, and that each god was attached in some way to some nation. No one ever thought of a god without a nation, and no one ever thought of the god of a nation exercising any moral authority over another nation. A god might assume authority over a conquered nation as the god of the conquerers, but every god's authority was limited by the boundaries of the nation over which it presided or by the force of the armies that went out to battle in its name.

When Amos announced that the pagan nations were judged by Yahweh on the basis of their moral acts it was a very great advance in religious thought, for it suggested that Yahweh was the God of all the earth and that all nations were responsible to him.

86 Was Amos correct in his analysis of conditions?

While he does not name Assyria as the foe that is to come down upon Israel, there can be little doubt that he recognized her as the threat to the whole world. The subsequent events of history vindicated his position entirely.

87 What was Amos' program?

He declared that Yahweh was altogether indifferent to their burning rams (5:21-27). Their shrines and their altars meant nothing to him (5:4-9). Their hope lay, not in sacrifices and ritual, but in righteous living, the administration of justice, and a complete repudiation of all social evils (5:14-15).

Just as in the days of David hired thugs and ruffians (*gibborim*) overran the country under commission as military police, so the government of Israel ruled by strong-arm methods. These, Amos declared, were to be crushed (2:14-15) and the whole despicable machine broken up. In this the prophet was expressing the long-pent-up bitterness of the small country farmers toward the rich exploiters who were in control of the capital.

88 Was Amos unreasonable?

It may not seem so to us, but to the people of the East it was revolutionary doctrine. It was as startling as if Amos should appear among us and say, "Your fine churches, your revival meetings, your missionary programs, and all your lavish services mean nothing to God. Nothing whatever! If you want to win his favor, then abolish your slums, stop your wars, readjust your wage scales, clean up your theaters, and put an end to racial discrimination!"

89   How did the people receive his message?

It was highly offensive to several groups whom he charged with being responsible for the nation's condition. The priests, the nobility, the women, the rich merchants, and the professional prophets all come in for scathing denunciation. Special mention was reserved for Amaziah, the priest, and Jeroboam, the king.

90   With what did he charge the priests?

He charged them with two failures: (1) he said that their emphasis upon ceremony, ritual, and sacrifice had misled the people (5:4-9, 14-15), and (2) he declared that their doctrine of the "Day of Jehovah" had blinded the nation to the dreadful fate that awaited it (5:19-20).

91   With what did he charge the nobility?

The nobles were the rich capitalists of the country, in whose hands there rested the economic and, in large part, the political destiny of the nation. Some of them had summer homes in Damascus and winter houses in Samaria. These were elaborate affairs, with rich furnishings and extravagant budgets. With multitudes of the plain people living in the most abject poverty, such ostentation was a gross sin, and Amos condemned it in unsparing terms (3:9, 11, 15; 5:5).

92   With what did he charge the women?

Their excessive demands upon their husbands had driven the men to further and more heartless oppression of the poor. In the region east of the Jordan there was a cattle-grazing country called Bashan, where stock was fattened for the market. The well-fed women in the congregation of worshipers reminded Amos of the sleek cattle of Bashan, and he launched out at them in a vitriolic attack that has no equal in the Old Testament (4:1-3).

93   With what did Amos charge the professional prophets?

Many of them were attached to Jeroboam's court as seers and magicians. It was their business to counsel the king and nobles on matters of public policy. What Amos had to say that day at the shrine was in direct contradiction to everything they had been saying, and if Amos were right then their whole profession was discredited. It was a serious situation for them in which their whole living was involved.

94 With what did he charge the merchants?

Keep in mind the fact that these were the speculators who manipulated the market and piled up the quick and easy fortunes. They were so intent upon making money that they chafed under the small restraints imposed upon them by the holidays connected with the religious feasts (8:5). They were so land greedy that they lusted for the dust that a poor country farmer poured on his head as a token of mourning in the presence of death (2:7); their business methods were so vicious that they employed a wide variety of subterfuges to cheat and rob the helpless poor (8:5-6).

95 What did Amos have to say to Amaziah?

In the midst of his speech he was interrupted by the priest in charge of the shrine, who charged him with being one the professional prophets trying to terrify the audience into paying him a bribe. It is not difficult to imagine the fat cleric, livid with rage, ordering him back to his own country of Judah, where the people would be glad to pay him for speaking fierce denunciations of Israel (7:12).

Amos hotly denied the accusation that he was one of the despised "sons of the prophets" and proclaimed the fact that he owed his message and his call directly to Yahweh himself. With terrible sternness he announced to Amaziah that he should suffer unendurable tragedy because of his failure to recognize the message as being from Yahweh, and because of his moral failure in leading the people astray. The protection of the king would be of no avail (7:14-17).

96 What did he have to say to the king?

Jeroboam II, king of Israel, was in the midst of a reign that was, in many respects, one of the most brilliant the little kingdom had ever known; but underneath its splendor Amos saw the exploited poor, the defenseless realm, and the betrayed kingdom. For much of the terrible doom descending upon the nation he held Jeroboam responsible (7:9) and freely predicted his death by the sword. This word against the royal house gave Amaziah his opportunity to interrupt the prophet.

97 Did Amos see no hope?

He declared boldly that their shrines and services were helpless to save them (5:21-23) and that guilt was widespread. But he was also of the opinion that there might be a pious minority, and upon such he pinned whatever hope he had (5:14-15). It would be a small, chewed-up remnant, to be sure; but it might survive (3:12).

98 Had the nation had any warning?

Though no other voice had been raised in warning, Amos pointed out that the nation had suffered drought, famine, blight, mildew, plague, and earthquakes (4:6-12), all of which should have been a sufficient warning. But so sure was he of the final fate that at one point in his address he dropped into a dirge, as if he were attending the funeral of the kingdom and were singing its death song (5:1-3).

99 What happened as a result of his speech?

Amaziah took the situation in hand, ordered him to keep silence, dispatched messengers to the king notifying him that treason had been uttered at the shrine, and apparently the prophet was hustled out of town. It is seldom true that a government founded on oppression dares to permit the full luxury of free speech, free press, or free assemblies.

100 Did amos accept his banishment?

Denied the privilege of speaking to the people, Amos seems to have returned to his home and committed his message to writing. It was probably circulated as a piece of undercover literature, being passed from hand to hand surreptitiously as a revolutionary document. This, of course, is nothing more than a surmise, for there is no word in the Old Testament which throws light on the matter. But at any rate Amos, in putting his convictions into writing, earned the high distinction of being the first man to write a complete book of the Bible.

101 Did the Bible begin then with a protest?

As we have already learned, there was other literature in existence at the time which finally found its way into the Bible; but the first book to be completed was the little book of prophecy by the humble shepherd of Tekoa. It was the protest of a poor countryman against the woeful wrongs under which the people were suffering at the hands of a political ring of money lords who were in control of the government.

Because the religious leaders allowed those wrongs to continue, he charged them with complicity in the crimes. Because the rich and noble classes participated in those evils, he charged them with being sinners. Because the nation was guilty of allowing such conditions, he predicted its downfall, declaring that God would never come to the rescue of a people who were not primarily concerned with the establishment of justice. "Let justice roll down . . . . like an ever-flowing stream," he shouted (5:24), and his cry has been echoed by crusaders for justice ever since that day.

102 Who was Hosea?

The second of the writing prophets of the eighth century B.C. and the only prophet from Israel whose writings are to be found in the Old Testament.

103 Who were the writing prophets?

There had been other prophets—true prophets such as Elijah and Elisha—who had appeared among the people and spoken in behalf of Yahweh, but we have no record of their sermons except that which was preserved for us in traditions and fragmentary records. With Amos, however, we come upon a new type of prophet—one who saw the value (perhaps under the force of necessity) of putting his message into writing that it might not die with him. There may have been other prophets who spoke out just as courageously at the same time, but of them we have no records. And the only reason why we know about Amos and his preaching is because he wrote his message down. In doing so he launched a precedent which has given us some of the greatest religious literature in existence.

104 When did Hosea preach?

A few years after Amos' appearance at Bethel, the exact date being unknown. It is believed, however, that his preaching career occurred during the closing days of the reign of Jeroboam II, and in the midst of the chaotic days that followed, down to about 736 B.C. Thus his ministry covered a considerable part of one of the painful periods of Hebrew history.

105 What was Hosea's background?

The fact that his father is mentioned (Hosea 1:1) would seem to indicate that he was a member of a family of some social importance, perhaps one of the small landed gentry. There is no information as to how he earned his living, which suggests that he may have lived off the income of a modest rural estate. He seems to have been a prophet all his adult life, and yet he was connected with no professional group. He was reared inside the little kingdom of Israel, and when he preached he was speaking to his own people. He dealt with them much more sympathetically than did Amos, for the Tekoan shepherd was brusque and harsh, while Hosea was gentle and affectionate. Amos referred to the nation as Joseph (Amos 5:6, 15; 6:60, whereas Hosea used the intimate and affectionate name Ephraim no less than thirty-six times. It is a little singular that he makes no such passionate defense of the poor as Amos did; but he seems to have been fully aware of the state of the nation, the dangers that threatened from without, and to have had a definite political policy for the government which he urged with all the powers at his command.

106 What was the state of religion in Israel?

Both Israel and Judah were Hebrew kingdoms, of course, and there was no great difference in the racial stock. But after the division of the kingdom the two nations followed entirely different lines of religious development.

The primitive religions of the East all centered about the idea of increase, as we have noted, and religious worship was practiced as an effort to cajole the gods (Baalim) into providing abundant crops and an increase of the herds. Religion and economics were always very closely allied. This resulted in an emphasis on the sex motif, which became the theme of religious worship.

It was a common practice for the Baal worshipers to present their daughters to the shrines as "wives of the gods." There they served as prostitutes, hired out to worshipers, their earnings going to the support of the shrine. It would be a mistake to think of this as being the same as modern commercialized vice, however, for the practice was circumscribed by certain restrictions which prevented it from being mere promiscuity. It was surrounded by the sanction of religion, and bore no stigma in the minds of the ancients.

107 What effect did this have on the Hebrews?

While the Hebrews lived in the wilderness they were simple nomads, and Yahweh was their God. The thought of Yahweh as a storm god, a god of battles, and as a protector; but not as an agricultural god because they themselves had no concern in agriculture.

When they moved out of the wilderness into the Land of Promise they faced the necessity of altering their whole way of life. Their living no longer depended upon good fortune in finding lush oases where water was in abundance and fruits and forage were provided. Now they must depend upon their own skill in planting, cultivating and harvesting—*and the uncontrollable factors of rainfall and soil fertility.*

Inasmuch as Moses had not taught them that other gods did not exist (only that they should have no other gods *before* Yahweh), it was easy to convince them that to worship the local gods of the soil was just good business. Therefore they built shrines for the *Baalim* alongside their altars to Yahweh. They were never far away from the temptation to mix paganism with Yahwehism.

108 How long did this condition last?

We find evidences of it all the way down through Hebrew history from the wilderness to the Exile (Judges 17:5; 18:14-20).

109 Did the Hebrews practice sacred prostitution?

Amos found it in vogue in Israel (Amos 2:7). It is impossible to know just to what extent it was practiced by the Hebrews, but that it went on inside the land is certain. The migrants from other lands brought it in with them and practiced it at the altars erected to their gods in various Hebrew cities. Hebrew women became enmeshed in the pagan systems in various ways, and it was impossible to tolerate it among the foreigners without its effects appearing among the Israelites themselves.

110 What part did Hosea play in this situation?

His earlier sermons seem to have been vigorous denunciations of the prevailing immoralities of the time. He was keenly sensitive to the sins of Israel and spoke out against them, sometimes with deep passion (Hosea, chapters 1-3). He condemned the political blunders of the government especially.

111 What were those political blunders?

As the Assyrian menace grew, the kingdom of Israel turned instinctively to Egypt for help. Egyptian diplomats, always at the courts of the small nations, made large promises in behalf of their home government in the hope that the little Palestinian states might serve as an effectual buffer holding the mighty Assyria at bay. Clearer than any other man in the kingdom Hosea saw the folly of such an alliance and denounced it with all his might (5:13; 7:11, 15; 8:9; 9:3; 12:1; 14:3). He seems to have recognized the duplicity of Egypt and the terrible might of the oncoming Assyrian, and he did all in his power to keep his king clear of entangling alliances with the nation which he so rightly judged to be a faithless ally. He could foresee that any such arrangement with Egypt would only anger the Assyrians and hasten the day when the land would be overrun.

112 Was Hosea a political preacher?

His first sermons were passionate pleas that the nation should keep clear of alliances. They dealt with political and international issues, but in every case Hosea announced what he believed to be the judgment of God. The turning point in his career, however, came in connection with a great domestic tragedy.

113 What was that domestic tragedy?

Hosea married a girl by the name of Gomer, the daughter of Diblaim (1:3). The mention of her father lends credence to the belief that she was the daughter of one of the small rural landed aristocrats. Sometime after her marriage to Hosea Gomer took up with the licentious rites practiced at the pagan shrines, and gave herself over as one of the sacred prostitutes. She was not sold into the life but entered of her own free will. It is quite possible that she did so for religious reasons, and perhaps the charge of viciousness should not be lodged against her. But the domestic tragedy was hardly lessened by any religious sanction it may have had in Gomer's mind. Nevertheless Hosea went on loving her, and when she was cast off by the shrine Hosea found her in a slave market and purchased her for the price of a slave, taking her into the country with the intention of wooing her back to virtue. The fact that he continued to love such a woman was something of a mystery to the prophet himself, but as he thought about the matter he came to the conclusion that if love such as his could exist for such a woman as Gomer, then surely the love of Jehovah must persist for such a nation as Israel. The tragedy of his own life caused him to see the sins of the nation in a new light. He came to understand that Jehovah loved Israel as he loved Gomer. With this new message he went out to preach to the nation again, this time of the love of Yahweh.

114 Why call it a new message?

His earlier sermons were full of bitterness and scathing indictments. He had seen the sin of the nation and poured out his wrath upon the people and their political leaders without mercy. But his own tragedy corrected his vision, and his later messages were models of tenderness and winsome love.

115 What are the facts of the marriage story?

1. The marriage to Gomer (1:2-3).
2. The birth of the first child, Jezreel (1:4-5).
3. The birth of the second child, Not pitied (1:6).
4. The birth of the third child, Not my people (1:9).
5. Gomer's search for other lovers (2:5).
6. The vain appeal of the children (2:2).
7. Gomer's self-confidence (5:15; 6;1-3).
8. Hosea finds her in the slave market (3:2).
9. He purchases her and takes her to the country (3:2-3).
10. The domestic tragedy is used as a text from which to preach to the nation that Jehovah will not give Israel up, even though it is necessary to punish her for her sins (3:4-5).

46

116 Why did Hosea marry such a woman?

There are two interpretations of this story. One is that God actually directed the prophet to marry her that he might teach the nation a lesson. The other is that Hosea married her and only discovered her true character after the third child was born. But either interpretation can be accepted without doing any damage to the central theme of the book—the message of love to the nation of Israel. The great teachings of Hosea revolve about this one thought—that the sine of the nation cannot alienate the love of God.

117 Why was the first child named Jezreel?

The Hebrew town of Jezreel was associated in history with some of the bloodiest chapters in the whole record of the kingdom of Israel (I Kings 16:33; 18:45-46; II Kings 8:29; 9:30-37; 10:7, 11), and the name was given to the child as a living sermon to the nation against militarism and the bloody house of Jehu whose descendant still sat upon the throne. It was a protest against the proposed alliance with Egypt and an appeal to the nation to remain neutral and keep out of the impending war. Hosea was announcing the doom of the nation because it had oppressed the poor and spilled their blood in fruitless wars.

118 Why was the second child named Not pitied?

The name indicates the message of unrelenting wrath which Hosea preached to the people at that period of his ministry. Scholars are divided in their opinion as to whether or not Hosea knew of his wife's infidelity at this time; but no matter which way the truth lies in the case the significance of the name remains the same. It is a sermon of stern judgment to a nation that shows no sign of repentance, and it represents the heart of the preacher as being bitter and unloving.

119 Why was the third child named Not my people?

Some have assumed the name to mean that Hosea was denying the child's paternity. But this can hardly have been the case. The name was a sermon of judgment—Yahweh has cast the people off because of their sin.

The idea of a chosen people was one of the major doctrines among the Hebrews, who believed that Yahweh had chosen them as a special people. No one had ever before presumed to suggest that they might be disowned. Hosea was trying to impress them with the fact that sinning was such terrible business that it was even capable of severing the ties that bound them to Yahweh, and the child's name was to be a sermon to that effect.

120 What were these terrible national sins?

According to the priests, as we learned in our study of Amos, sin was nothing worse than an incorrect performance of a ritual. But according to Amos and Hosea the sins of the nation were economic, social, and political misdeeds. In his earlier ministry Hosea does not mention specific sins, but in his later sermons he makes bold and vigorous attacks on the stupid policies of the nation (6:4; 7:11; 8:4; 9:6) and calls them outright sins.

121 Was Hosea correct in his interpretation of his times?

Less than twenty years after Hosea closed his ministry the northern kingdom of Israel ceased to exist. The Assyrians came down in force, sacked the capital of Samaria, and carried 27,290 persons off into Assyrian captivity. The nation therewith passed off the stage of history, never again to appear as a political unit, and for the very reason that Hosea had declared—a combination of corrupt religion and debauched politics.

122 Why was Israel's religion so corrupt?

For generations the priests had taught the people that Yahweh would care for them no matter what happened, if they were faithful in their performance of the ceremonies. They had met those conditions with great care, and yet the nation fell. When disaster overtook them their faith went crumbling along with the walls of their capital. The theory of the priests simply did not work. The reputation of the priests and religious leaders suffered a staggering blow and their doctrines were repudiated. The events of history had disproven everything the priests had taught, and they had no new solution. A religion of ceremony and ritualism does not produce prophets—it only breeds priests.

123 Why is the story of Gomer so important?

If the story of Hosea had contained nothing to teach except the tragedy of one man's marriage, the book would never have been preserved for us as scripture. But out of the catastrophic domestic experience one man came to an understanding of the great fact that God is capable of amazing love. Amos somehow discovered God's concern for justice; and Hosea, when he found there was love in his own heart for Gomer in spite of her infidelity, caught a glimpse of the undefeatable love God had for the nation.

124 Is this the beginning of the doctrine of love?

This is the first record we have in the Scriptures of the love of God as an essential quality of his nature and character. We must keep in mind, however, that it is love for the nation and not love for the individual sinner.

125 Why is it not also love for the individual?

Because the idea of personal religion, with divine love bestowed upon individuals, had not yet come to birth. It was a hundred years later, through the sermons of Jeremiah, that this enlarged concept of God was preached. Individuals as members of the nation might benefit by the love of God, but only as members of the nation and not as individuals. Hosea's doctrine of love was a national, not an individual, matter.

126 Did Hosea have no individual message?

Like Amos, Hosea nowhere in his book discusses the individual's relationship with God. There is nothing in it that speaks about personal immortality, salvation, communion, prayer, or personal spiritual experience. As we read the book we must always keep in mind the fact that Hosea is thinking in national, not personal, terms.

127 How did Hosea discover the love of God?

The details of his mental and spiritual processes are not revealed in his writing. He is content to tell us the result at which he arrived rather than the route or process by which he came. Sometime, we know not when or how, as Hosea meditated on the miracle of his own love for an erring wife it became clear to him that this was also the way God loved an erring nation. So far as we know there was no vision, no trance, and no ecstatic experience of any kind. Life had struck him a terrible blow, and that blow had so awakened him that he understood the heart of the Infinite. To Christians of this modern day, instructed by Jesus, the explanation is perfectly plain: the Holy Spirit of the Living God used the experience to reveal this great truth to the honest and open-minded prophet.

128 How did Gomer's sin parallel the nation's sin?

Just as Gomer had sunk to the level of her paramours, so Israel had sunk to the level of the surrounding paganism (4:6-9). Just as Gomer always assumed she could come back to her home at any time without repentance, so the nation had presumed on the love of God (5:15; 6:1-3; 7:13; 10:13-14). Just as Gomer had been a silly fool, so Israel had played with her destiny (6:4; 7:11; 8:4; 9:6). Gomer had sinned sordidly and Israel had wasted her heritage (4:1-3).

129 Where did the responsibility lie?

Hosea had expected great things from Jeroboam, but instead he had found debauchery and dissolution. His country neighbors might be idol worshipers, but they were honest; whereas the worshipers of Yahweh, so far as the paganized cities were concerned, were corrupt in their hearts (4:1-2). The complacence of the self-righteous in Samaria stirred him deeply (12:9). In the rural districts he talked with yokels who might not be expected to think in large terms, but in the capital he found them equally incapable of high thinking. The priests were all deaf to such preaching.

130 What was really wrong with the government?

Using the name Ephraim, a very tender title, Hosea pictured the nation as being corrupt from top to bottom (7:3 ff.), and in this he found the explanation why Israel entered first one foolish treaty after another which could not possibly be kept (7:11; 12;1).

131 What about public morals?

The youth of the land were consorting with harlots, and to

Hosea there was no difference between masculine and feminine immorality. This single standard represented a very great advance for the Orient. He saw pagan idolatry as the root of it all (4:17; 8:5-6; 12:11). The whole nation was hopelessly corrupt (chapter 4), and for this dreadful state of affairs he held the priests largely responsible (4:4-10). Corruption, adultery, drunkenness, conspiracies, and assassinations were commonplace (7:1-7).

132 What did Hosea believe about God?

He believed in one God (3:5; 8:4; 13:2; 14:3) whose power extended to other nations as well as to Israel, and—like Amos in this respect—he had no hope of winning the favor of Yahweh through ritual and ceremony. The only way to be sure of Yahweh's help, so far as he could see, was by righteous conduct and purity of life. But Hosea's doctrine of love made it logical for him to assert that a nation, even after it had sinned, could be sure of the love of Yahweh if it showed any signs of penitence, though he thought in terms of Israel only, and held out no offer of hope to any other nation.

133 Did Hosea know he was writing scripture?

No more than Amos did, at least so far as anything in his writing would indicate. Again it must be noted that the idea of scripture had not yet come to birth. So far as we can discover in his book, he had not the slightest thought that he was writing for any generation except his own. His messages were the product of a great spiritual conviction, a desperate national situation, a heartbreaking personal tragedy, and an inspired understanding of the nature and character of God.

134 Who was Isaiah?

He was another of the great writing prophets of the eighth century B.C. and the most sublime of them all. In the length of his public life, the importance of his message, the significance of his service, the originality of his thought, the literary skill with which he wrote, the discernment with which he analyzed the problems of his times, and his unique qualities as a statesman, Isaiah easily takes rank as one of the half-dozen greatest Hebrews of all time.

135 Where did he preach?

He was a resident, and probably a native, of Jerusalem. So far as we can discover he was never outside of the kingdom of Judah, and only on a few occasions outside of Jerusalem. In all this he occupies a peculiar position in Hebrew religion and politics.

136 In what sense is he peculiar?

Tradition has it that he was related to the king, but of that we have no confirmation. Certainly, however, he had been reared in the midst of the paganism of Jerusalem, with its imported altars, divinities, and rituals, and was familiar through daily contact with the political machine which ruled the land. Yet in spite of his privileged position he became one of the most severe critics of the government and of the social system that his day produced.

137 When did he minister to the nation?

It is impossible to fix the exact day on which he was born, but he says that "in the year that king Uzziah died" (6:10 he was called to his ministry by a vision that came to him in the Temple at Jerusalem. Though there is some small disagreement among historians, the year 740 B.C. can probably be taken as the date of Uzziah's death and the beginning of the prophet's spectacular career. We know that his ministry extended at least a short time beyond 700 B.C., which means that he was active through one of the most disastrous periods in all Hebrew history.

138 To whom did he prophesy?

During the early years of his ministry Isaiah addressed his sermons to both Israel and Judah, condemning their sins in the most vigorous manner. But in the year 721 B.C. the city of Samaria fell, and though some small resistance was offered to the Assyrians thereafter, Isaiah confined his interests and ministry to Judah. But throughout his long career as a preacher, and during his later years as confidential adviser of kings, he was immersed in the political movements of his day.

139 Was Isaiah a politician?

Not in the sense that he was an office seeker, for he had no aspirations in that direction. But as one who was interested in the welfare of the nation he was primarily a politician. He was living at a time when all politics were world politics, when the policy of every nation was, in some way, linked up with world affairs. No one could take an interest in the destiny of his own people and ignore the significance of world movements.

140 Was Isaiah a professional prophet?

He was not. In fact, by social standing, training, and spiritual interest he was as far removed from the professional prophetic class as any man of his generation could have been. It is true that he saw a vision in the Temple and that that vision sent him out to prophesy; but unlike the professional prophets who relied upon trances, visions, and ecstatic states to convince the people of their prophetic status, Isaiah does not seem to have mentioned his Temple experiences until some years afterward, when his ministry was far along (chapter 6).

141 What was his social position?

He seems to have been a member of a family of some social standing because his father's name is mentioned, and the fact that his home was in Jerusalem would suggest that he belonged to the wealthy aristocracy of the capital (1:1). He had plenty of time for his prophetic work, and, since he makes no mention of any trade or profession by which he might have earned a livelihood, it is easy to believe that he was a man of leisure, with an independent income.

142 What was the political situation in Israel?

Amos preached at Bethel about 750 B.C., when the Assyrian invasion was still in the future. Hosea preached during those riotous years just before the final crash, when one ruling house of Israel was plunging headlong to its destruction. But Isaiah preached in Judah while the Assyrians were on their way, and then a few years later at the very moment they were breaking through the walls of Samaria. His closing ministry occurred during one of the most terrible episodes in all the long history of Jerusalem, when the little kingdom of Judah was threatened with destruction and saved itself only at the price of complete vassalage.

For almost one hundred years prior to the beginning of Isaiah's ministry Judah had been but little more than a vassal of Israel, but under the leaderhip of Uzziah something like independence had been achieved. In Jeroboam II of Israel and Uzziah of Judah the Hebrew people had two of the most competent kings in all their histories. In campaigns north and south Jeroboam had made Israel secure (II Kings 14:25), extending its borders and strengthening its internal defenses. Everywhere there was a feeling of confidence and faith in the future. The lavish sacrifices at the shrines were an expression of this general sense of security (Amos 4:4; 5:5, 21-23).

Jeroboam died in 747 B.C., and for twenty-five years thereafter Israel was plagued with a succession of civil wars, uprisings, usurpations, and revolts which seated six different kings upon the throne, their reigns characterized by violence, rioting, and demoralization. During those days Hosea preached, as we have seen.

Something of a parallel situation existed in Judah, with Uzziah on the throne, except that the government itself was a stable one and undisturbed by rioting. The king encouraged agriculture, expended considerable sums on public works, expanded the kingdom, made the borders secure, and developed trade and commerce. Certainly he was one of the most popular monarchs the little kingdom had seen upon the throne since the days of David.

143 What was the situation in Egypt?

The land of the Nile was torn by internal dissension. Egypt continued active in diplomacy and intrigue, but her government was never able to fulfill the promises her representatives abroad made for her. Her strength was dissipated between contending factions at home, and her treasure was absorbed in her own internal strife. She had but one main purpose—to keep the peace behind her own borders and to keep the Palestinian states fighting her battles abroad.

144 What was the situation in Assyria?

Throughout most of the first half of the eighth century B.C. the Empire was fully occupied with border troubles and internal disorders. Through three successive reigns incompetent rulers sat upon the throne content to leave well enough alone. But in

745 B.C., two years after the death of Jeroboam II, and about five years before the death of Uzziah, Tiglath Pileser III came to the throne and began to lay plans for the conquest of the world. When Isaiah began his ministry the Assyrian Empire was in a ferment of excitement and preparations for war.

145 What was the situation in Judah?

Edom, an ancient border rival, had been brought under subjection (II Kings 14:7) and a port on the Red Sea had been taken (II Kings 14:22) which enabled Uzziah to work the copper mines of the Arabah with some profit. Commerce flourished, producing great wealth and great wrongs (Isaiah 2:7, 17; 3:14; 5:11, 14, 22 ff.). An extensive agricultural program was launched with the caravan routes well policed and the rural areas provided with cisterns and fortifications. The military forces of the nation were trained and well equipped (II Chronicles 26:11-15).

During the last years of Uzziah's life the king was a victim of leprosy, and the crown prince, Jotham, sat upon the throne (II Kings 15:5-7). Uzziah's illness created two problems of major proportions. According to the thinking of the times it was agreed that his illness was a result of some terrible sin. But he had been a devout king, up to the time of his illness, and his reign had seen great prosperity. These two conflicting facts created much confusion in the minds of the people. How could prosperity and ill favor with Jehovah go together?

In the second place the absence of the king's strong hand at the helm of the government resulted in a general deterioration. The military organization began to disintegrate. Some effects could be noticed in the commercial life of the land, and the general confusion undermined the unity of the nation. In the midst of this restless and disturbed period Isaiah saw his vision in the Temple and launched his career as a prophet. But the nation was in no mood to listen to a prophet who preached as Isaiah did. Because of the very nature of his message—warning and condemnation—the spirit of the times was against him.

146 Why did Isaiah become a prophet?

No other prophet of the Old Testament is more explicit in giving the facts than is Isaiah. He tells his story frankly and in detail.

Nothing is known of his life up to the time of his call but we can guess from his own statements that he was a fashionable young man about town who lived the usual carefree life of a rich and aristocratic youth (Isaiah 6:5).

Perhaps with the feeling that some great international disaster was impending, he went to the Temple to pray. It was the last year of Uzziah's life (740 B.C.); and it may have been that he, like the rest of the nation, was perplexed by the dilemma presented by the case of a devout and prosperous king who suffered from leprosy—a symbol of divine displeasure. At any rate his story of the Temple vision is very graphic.

He saw a thrilling vision of chorusing angels, a glistening throne, and an awe-inspiring spectacle of supernatural glory (6:1-11). In the midst of the vision he heard God calling for help and he volunteered his services (6:8). Thereupon he was commissioned to preach to the people and at the same time he was warned that they would not listen to him.

One of the greatest careers ever experienced by any Hebrew began with that vision. Throughout his life, with the exception of a few last hard years, he was in the minority. Aware of titanic events about the occur, and sensing a crack-up of civilization, he preached and no one listened. The professional prophets attacked him; the priests fought him bitterly; the government refused to listen to his counsel and kings rejected his advice; and all the time he watched the nation slipping lower and lower, nearing the awful abyss. But history has vindicated him, and millions now turn hungrily to his words that their faith may be restored.

147 How did he begin his ministry?

His first sermons were preached before the Assyrian war machine actually began to roll across Palestine. To the superficial observer all might have seemed well with the little kingdoms. Prosperity was everywhere evident. The borders of the kingdoms were unimpaired. The shrines were crowded and the sacrifices piled high.

But the worship of Yahweh was well-nigh supplanted by the paganism which had come in with the caravans, and Isaiah's first sermons indicted the nations for their idolatry (2:10 ff.).

It would have been almost impossible for anyone to mingle with the crowds of merchants, travelers, and traders in the market place without detecting the symptoms of impending world struggle. Gossip of world events was on everyone's lips.

A sense of approaching disaster developed within the mind of the prophet. He knew that the nation's leaders were corrupt (3:1, 12), high-born citizens took no responsibility for the affairs of the state, allowing them to drift into the hands of the machine (3:6-8), and graft was common (3:14-15). Social life was thoughtless and superficial (3:16), and no one in authority seemed aware of the hideous dangers that threatened (3:17-24). There were times when he was so oppressed with the tragedy that lay ahead of the nation that his indignation ran riot, and he anticipated the time when seven women would clamor for the favors of one man, so depleted would the nation be in manpower.

Those early sermons were general in tone, condemnatory in spirit, social and political in their implications, and courageous in their manner and matter. But it was the crisis of 734 B.C. that ushered him into his real career as a prophet-statesman.

148   What happened in 734 B.C.?

When Tiglath Pileser III came to the throne of Assyria in 745 B.C. he immediately became the greatest political fact in the world. The political policy of every other nation was fashioned by the things he did and the plans he laid. With the might of Assyria behind him no nation in the East dared ignore him. He held the initiative and was capable of producing all the military surprises.

Through the first few years of his reign he organized the Empire's military forces until they became the greatest war machine the world had ever known. By bold strokes, rapid moves, forced marches, and military miracles, he soon had the stage set for an invasion of Egypt.

The envoys of Egypt were likewise feverishly active during this same period. Back and forth across the deserts they raced with glib promises of aid, bribes offered in exchange for resistance to Assyria, and extravagant assurances of help in emergencies. Egypt probably was least deluded of all as to the possibility of an invasion.

Then the mighty machine began rolling. In 743 B.C. Tiglath Pileser loosed his terrific blows on Syria and Israel, and by 738 B.C. both little kingdoms were paying him tribute though they still remained intact. An internal uprising called the Assyrian back east for a time and gave the Palestinian states two or three precious years in which to organize effective resistance.

The first shock of Assyrian arms was severe enough to convince Syria and Israel that they must forget their ancient differences and unite in the common cause. Thereupon Rezin, the king of Syria, and Pekah, who had fought his way to the throne of Israel on an Anti-Assyrian platform, set up an alliance in 734 B.C. and demanded that Judah should join them.

149 What was the situation in Judah?

Ahaz had just come to the throne as a youth of twenty, and he was altogether unprepared either by training or by temperament for the vast responsibilities that were suddenly thrust upon him (II Chronicles 28:1). Moreover, he was entirely inexperienced in war or administration. No one knows why, but for some reason the young king turned deaf ears to the appeals of Syria and Israel; and the two allies immediately organized an expedition against Judah for the purpose of putting Tabeal's son upon the throne (Isaiah 7:6), thus to insure the nation's co-operation in their alliance against Assyria. Edom in the east, quick to see the plight of Judah, revolted (II Kings 16:6; II Chronicles 28:17) and seized the seaport of Elath on the Red Sea and the coveted copper mines of the Arabah. Thus the commercial prosperity of Judah came to an end. In the midst of the crisis Isaiah came to the fore and began his political career.

150 What part did Isaiah play in the crisis?

Perhaps five years before, a son had been born to Isaiah to whom the symbolic name of "Shear-jashub" was given (meaning "a remnant will return"). This little lad, like the children of the prophet Hosea (Hosea 1:4, 6, 9), had gone about as a living sermon.

In 734 B.C. the armies of Pekah and Rezin appeared before the walls of Jerusalem, and the city was in a panic. Ahaz, the king, was probably worse terrified than any man in his kingdom, and in frantic fear was making tardy last-minute efforts to put the capital into a condition to withstand a siege.

Telling about it years afterward, Isaiah said that God instructed him to take the child with him as he went in search of the king to warn him against compromising with allies (7:3). The child with the strange name was to be a sermon to the king. The fact that Ahaz would have known the child, his name, and its significance, indicates that Isaiah was well known at the court.

The king had gone to inspect the city's water supply and was at the reservoir when Isaiah found him. There the prophet made an impassioned plea that the king stand firm, keep free from any entangling alliances, and allow Yahweh to defend the city (Isaiah 7).

151 Was Isaiah's policy a wise one?

Judah was a small kingdom set back among the hills. If the Assyrians should set out to invade Egypt the armies would march down the great trade route that skirted the sea, and would never cross Judah's border. If Ahaz kept out of the alliance it was possible that Assyria would inflict no worse injury than a few foraging forays, for there was less in Judah to tempt a raider than in any of the Palestinian states.

152 What was Ahaz' reaction?

The king was a weakling with no serious convictions on any subject, least of all on religion. Because he was ignorant, it was hard to reason with him. Because he lacked religious faith, it was impossible to appeal to his conscience. Two men could hardly have been found who differed more widely in the fundamental principles of their lives.

153 What program did Isaiah offer?

He seems to have understood the situation very well indeed. He described the two besieging kings as burnt-out firebrands (7:4) whose enmity could not possibly be dangerous (7:7-9). He was sure that if Ahaz would hold out against them long enough they would be compelled to turn back to defend their own borders, for Assyria could be expected to strike at any time. The prophet's policy was to sit tight, resist the siege, and await developments.

154 What did Isaiah do?

When the prophet saw he was making no impression he ventured on a daring course. Throwing all caution to the winds, and risking everything on one grand adventure of faith, he challenged the king to ask from him some sign. He was so sure he had the backing of Yahweh, and he was so positive he was speaking only those things which he had been commissioned to speak, that he staked everything on a single proposition. *Let the king ask for any sign—in heaven or earth—and Isaiah would produce it with God's help, just to prove to Ahaz that he was dealing with God and not with the prophet* (7:11).

155 Did the king accept the challenge?

He pretended modesty and said he would not tempt Yahweh (7:12); but the probabilities are that he had so far committed himself to the Assyrian alliance that he could not turn back, and did not want to be embarrassed by knowing the truth. Thereupon Isaiah announced that he would give him a sign anyhow.

156 What was that sign?

"A young woman shall conceive and bear a son," said Isaiah, "and shall call his name Immanuel." This child was to be a symbol to the king and to the people that Yahweh was their defender, for "Immanuel" means "God is with us." "Before the child knows how to refuse the evil and choose the good," the prophet went on, "the land before whose two kings you are in dread will be deserted" (7:14, 16).

157 What was the outcome?

In 733 B.C. Pekah, king of Israel, had been dragged from his throne and Hoshea (not to be confused with Hosea the prophet), a puppet, had been set up in his place. In 732 B.C., just one year later, Rezin, king of Syria, was executed and his kingdom wrecked.

158 What happened to Judah?

Ahaz' appeal for help had been accompanied by a huge bribe (II Kings 16:7 ff.) which had stripped the Temple and the royal palace of their treasures. This had turned the Assyrian aside, but Judah's safety had been purchased at the price of vassalage. Thereafter the little kingdom was under the necessity of paying a terrible toll to the Assyrian every year—an obligation that soon began to sap the strength of the country. But an even worse thing struck at the roots of the national religion.

159 **How was the religion of Judah affected?**

Immediately that Tiglath Pileser was successful in breaking up the revolt, Ahaz set out to visit him for the purpose of congratulating him on the victory and arranging the terms of the vassalage. At the Damascus headquarters of the Emperor, where the conference was held, whether at the command of Tiglath Pileser or because of a desire to compliment him, Ahaz ordered an altar to be constructed after the pattern of one found in Damascus, and sent it forward to be set up in the Temple at Jerusalem as a symbol of Assyria's overlordship. Having accepted Assyria's political authority, they had also to accept Assyrian divinities (II Kings 16:10 ff.).

160 **Did Judah turn to paganism?**

It was inevitable that the example of Ahaz and the presence of the pagan altar should have considerable effect upon the religious life and practices of the nation, and the further fact that Ahaz actually burned his own son as a fire offering (II Kings 16:3) indicates how deeply the apostasy went.

161 **What did Isaiah do about this?**

There was little he could do under the circumstances; but he preached a few sermons in which he expressed the opinion that Ahaz had prepared for himself and for the nation a terrible disaster from which there could be no escape (Isaiah 8:6-8a), and he turned about to take perhaps the most important step in his career.

162 **What was the most important step in his career?**

On the occasion of his call he had been warned that he would speak and that the nation would not listen. In this crisis he had come to realize the full and discouraging significance of that promise. It may have been that he thought his call to prophesy had ended and that he was at liberty to take up a new line of action. He therefore organized his followers into a group which is known to historians as the "prophetic party."

163 **What was the prophetic party?**

Naturally, the prophet had drawn to himself a number of

like-minded people who shared his confidence in Yahweh. To these he expounded his views (8:16) and taught his principles (chapter 8). Long after his death they carried on, eventually becoming the nucleus around which the spiritual life of the nation rallied for self-preservation.

164 **What about the movement?**

There is no evidence on the basis of which we can assert anything more than that it was a body of opinion which was opposed to the prevailing policy of the government. In no nation of antiquity had there been accorded so much freedom of speech and movement to critics of the government, in spite of the fact that repressive measures were often used (e.g., Amos). Prophets had been frank and candid. It was in such an atmosphere that the idea of the "opposition party" began, and in it was much of the spirit of Protestantism.

165 **How could it be called Protestant?**

The prophetic party proceeded on the principle that individuals had the right to hold an opinion, differing from that of the party in power. Holding such an opinion, they believed they had the right to organize for the sake of propagating their idea by seeking, through peaceable means, to establish it in the thinking of the nation. In this we have all the essentials of Protestantism—the right of individual opinion, and the independence of the individual believer.

166 **Did the prophetic party prosper?**

As we proceed in our study of the Old Testament we will discover that in time it exercised a very significant influence and that it was responsible for some extremely important religious developments. It would be a mistake, of course, to think that it was organized as a modern church, with officers, constitution, treasury, and meeting place. It was, rather, a group of congenial spirits whose ideas were more or less similar and who worked together for a common end.

167 **Was Isaiah the leader?**

There is no question about the fact that he initiated the movement; but just how far he can be said to have taken active leadership it is impossible to state, though that would be a natural inference. From the fact that a silent period ensues, following this experience, it seems probable that he concluded that his prophetic career was at an end and retired at least temporarily from the public scene. It would have been easy for him to believe that he had fulfilled his mission and ended his work. But the political situation in the East, always restless and agitated, did not allow him much respite. Soon he was thrust back into the scene again.

168   What happened to stir him up?

The Assyrian invasion of 732 B.C. was only the precursor of other expeditions; and in 721 B.C. the city of Samaria, after a brave resistance of three years, was finally captured and 27,290 leading citizens were carried off into captivity. It is a very strange but interesting fact that, so far as we can discover, we have no word from Isaiah concerning this tremendous event, for the fall of Samaria could not fail to shake Judah to her foundations. It is true, of course, that some scholars profess to find references to this tragic event in some of Isaiah's sermons, but such are debatable at best. Certainly there is nothing that can be positively identified as coming from that period.

169   What happened in Judah after Israel's fall?

When Ahaz sent his messengers to Assyria pleading for help, he committed his nation to a term of vassalage which continued, with exceptions of very short intervals, for one hundred and fifty years. During that time the land was thoroughly impoverished and the people suffered severely.

Ahaz died in 725 B.C., only a few years before the fall of Samaria, and was succeeded on the throne by his son, Hezekiah. The young king was patriotic, ambitious, and resentful under the Assyrian yoke bequeathed to him by his father. But the terrible havoc worked on Syria and Israel prevented him from taking any action, and year after year he paid the tribute with such grace as he could summon for the disagreeable task. Some of the other kinglets of Palestine were not so cautious.

170   What did otler kings propose?

In 720 B.C., just a year after the fall of Samaria, rebellion broke out among some of the other provinces, supported by an Egyptian army. In this case some few remaining Israelite warriors joined, in stubborn determination to avenge the destruction of their great capital and happy land. But Sargon, the new king of Assyria, struck back savagely and the revolt failed. In 713 B.C. an upstart seized the throne of Ashdod, one of the small city-states near the Mediterranean, and undertook to arouse the other small states to resist Assyrian aggression. The rebel leader was quickly overpowered and the effort failed. To the credit of Hezekiah let it be said that he held aloof from this abortive effort. But the possibility of involvement in the uprising stirred Isaiah to speak out of his retirement, and as a warning against further participation in war the prophet did one of the most daring and spectacular things of his whole life.

171 What was that dramatic activity?

Well aware of the war-mindedness of many in the government party, and just as well aware of the folly of such a course, Isaiah determined on a dramatic effort to stop the war. No one knew better than he did the complete inability of the small nations to resist the enormous power of Assyria. He was equally well aware of the worthlessness of Egypt's promises. He therefore counseled acceptance of Assyrian vassalage, hard and onerous as its conditions might be. He had witnessed the destruction of Israel, but he hoped for the survival of Judah, though she was independent in name only. Therefore, in an effort to make his plea for acceptance of the hard terms of Assyria effective, he stripped off his aristocratic garments and for three years went about the streets of Jerusalem, and throughout the surrounding villages, naked like a slave (20:3-5). Thus did he preach his opposition to the war program of the government (28:14-15).

172 Was he successful?

We have no way of knowing how far Hezekiah may have been influenced by Isaiah's opinion, nor can we know how much the public may have been moved. But at least Judah did not go to war. And then, within the space of a very few years, the Babylonian situation became serious.

173 Who were the Babylonians?

They were an ancient people who had experienced various political fortunes, and who lived along the lower ends of the Tigris and Euphrates valleys on the broad level plains. Theirs was a very old civilization and a reasonably high culture. In Amos' day they had been a part of the Assyrian Empire, paying tribute like the rest of the East. In 722 B.C. Shalmaneser V was putting forth every effort to breach the walls of Samaria when he was overtaken by death and was succeeded on the throne by Sargon, whose realm got out of hand while he was attempting to settle the Samaritan matter. One of the subject nations to take advantage of the Emperor's troubles was Babylon, led for the moment by a young patriot named Merodach-Baladan. He succeeded in establishing himself in a position of some power from which Sargon was never quite able to dislodge him. Then in 705 B.C. Sargon died and Babylon's big chance arrived.

174 What was the Babylonian policy?

Merodach-Baladan, having ridden into power in the midst of the confusion attending the death of Shalmaneser (722 B.C.), took full advantage of the confusion that followed the death of Sargon (705 B.C.); but the full measure of his success depended in no small part upon whatever help he was able to get from the Palestinian states. To further that end he penetrated the West with his diplomatic corps and made Judah an especial target.

175 How could the West help?

Between Babylon and Palestine lay the great Arabian Desert, with its vast stretches of waterless wastes, across which an army might move with the greatest difficulty. The two nations, Judah and Babylon, were located at the opposite ends of the Fertile Crescent, and yet they had a very great deal in common. Both were under the heel of Assyria; both were paying heavy tribute; both were smarting under the goading conditions of their vassalage; neither was strong enough to hope to overthrow Assyria without help. It was impossible for the two powers to march into the battle together; but if each made war on Assyria at the same time it would create fronts on both sides of the Empire, divide the Assyrian forces, and greatly increase the chances of success. Merodach's strategy then was to get the western powers organized and the attack timed. To that end he sent his diplomats abroad.

176 Was he able to work out his plan?

For the moment circumstances played well into his hands. Hezekiah was suffering a temporary illness and was in the convalescent stage. Under the pretext of sending him congratulations, Merodach-Baladan dispatched an envoy to Judah to lay the plan of revolt before the king and, if possible, secure his co-operation. It was a simple case of the strategy of the "second front." It is reasonable to assume that he sent other messengers to other courts, but of their success we know nothing, and besides the story does not need to go further than Hezekiah and the kingdom of Judah. It was the visit of the Babylonian envoys that called Isaiah into action again.

177 What did they have to do with Isaiah?

The prophet evidently enjoyed the favor of the king, with access to the royal apartment (perhaps because of royal connections). At any rate he was a more or less welcome visitor to the palace during the king's illness (II Kings 20; Isaiah 38), and on the occasion of one such call he discovered the presence of the Babylonians. This alarmed him greatly and he suspected that intrigue was going on.

178 Did he take any action?

Waiting for his first opportunity with such patience as he could muster, the prophet finally presented himself before the king and charged him with having connived with the Babylonians (Isaiah 39:5-7). It was a serious charge and if true it might jeopardize the safety of the entire kingdom.

179 What was Hezekiah's answer?

The king assured the prophet that he had made no commitments of any kind (39:8) but he did admit that he had shown the Babylonians the royal treasures.

180 What harm was there in that?

The envoys had come to congratulate Hezekiah on his recovery, and evidently they did with extravagant promises and compliments, profuse flattery, and ingratiating insinuations. Having won his confidence it was comparatively easy to persuade him to let them see the inner chambers of the royal palace and the national treasury. It was an extremely stupid thing for even a childish king to do, for it put the Babylonians into possession of every Hebrew secret, and the reports carried back to Babylon put Judah at the mercy of Merodach-Baladan.

181 Did Hezekiah have much to show?

In spite of the fact that the little land had no mineral resources and never was intended to support a people lavishly, the trade that crossed the Land of Promise did put considerable wealth within reach of the Hebrew kings; and in the temple, the royal palace, and other public buildings Judah had accumulated some precious and valuable things. Foremost among Hezekiah's treasures were stores of gold, silver, bronze, and precious stones. The golden vessels of the Temple were worth a king's ransom, and to a conqueror who was as badly in need of funds as Merodach-Baladan was the knowledge of Hezekiah's treasures could not have failed to be a temptation.

182 What was Judah's attitude toward the revolt?

There were three political parties in Judah. One was all for the revolt. This party consisted of the rural landowners, upon whom the burden of taxes fell most heavily because the rich members of the government machine were able to pass the burden on to them. Another party was in favor of an alliance with Egypt, its plans for the revolt corresponding very closely to those of the first party. But it was made up mostly of rich capitalists in Jerusalem who were exposed to Egyptian intrigue. Yet one other party was to be reckoned with—the prophetic party under the leadership of Isaiah, which was opposed to any alliance with an outside power, and which counseled acceptance of the Assyrian terms, hard as they were. Against the nobles who favored the Egyptian alliance Isaiah spoke out sharply (30:1-3, 6-7), reminding them of the hollowness of all promises that came from the region of the Nile. They, in turn, reprimanded Isaiah in vigorous terms (30:11), which moved him to make a second historic decision.

183 What was that second decision?

The criticism of the pro-Egyptian nobles so stirred Isaiah (30:13-14) that he determined to make a written record of his activities and attitudes so that posterity might judge of his wisdom and loyalty in the crisis (30:8); and to this decision we owe the existence of the book in the Old Testament which bears his name.

184 Did he write scripture?

It is a fact that he did write scripture, but he did not write it for scripture. As in the case of Amos and Hosea, the idea of scripture was not yet born, and no man of that period wrote anything with the thought that it would ever be scripture.

185 Was the revolt a success?

The new Assyrian monarch, Sennacherib, was an energetic ruler who knew the advantage of swift action. Merodach-Baladan was forced to flee; a puppet was set upon the throne; and then the Assyrian turned west to deal with the coconspirators. It was at this point that Isaiah reached one of his historic convictions which he formulated into a doctrine that was to rest at the foundation of Hebrew thought for more than a hundred years.

186 What did Sennacherib have to do with his conviction?

No one knew the wickedness of the heart of Assyria any better than Isaiah did. The tales of her atrocities and barbarities had been his daily fare since his earliest recollection. But suddenly Isaiah came to the conviction that, wicked though the Empire was, it had been chosen by Jehovah as the rod with which Judah was to be chastened. When she had been so used then God would turn and deal with Assyria according to her deserts (10:5-27). In his imagination the prophet saw Assyria marching on Jerusalem (10:28-32); yet he was not afraid, for *he believed that the city of Jerusalem would never be destroyed!*

Was not the capital the dwelling place of Jehovah? Could Jehovah allow Jerusalem to be destroyed without suffering irreparable loss of prestige? Would Jehovah allow profane hands to be laid upon that holy place? It became central in Isaiah's belief that Jerusalem was inviolate (10:33-34), and this conviction gathered strength with the succeeding years and experience.

It was not that Judah alone was to be punished for her sins, but the surrounding nations were to feel the harsh hand of Yahweh also (14:24-27), for they were all guilty. Isaiah believed the deliverance would not come by force of arms, but by the direct intervention of Yahweh (9:2, 4, 6-7). In this we have an expression of his deep faith which was probably his most outstanding characteristic.

187 What about Isaiah's faith?

His concept of faith is to be found in two passages (7:1-9; 28:16). Contrasted with his neighbors who had a form of faith which rested back on military power (2:7, 15; 31:1), human shrewdness (5:21; 29:14 f.; 31:2), and magic (2:6, 8), Isaiah believed implicitly in the character and dependability of God. We would say today that he had a supreme confidence in the moral order of the universe. He was sure that help would come from God and that it could not possibly come from the popular idols.

188 What was the prophet's foreign policy?

In every crisis he had been opposed to entangling alliances, favoring no coalition with any power. Whenever Judah made a treaty he believed it should be kept, but he was opposed to making them in the first place if they involved war. He was a strict isolationist in a world where neutrality was difficult and where any kind of an alliance meant vassalage. He believed in Yahweh with a complete and an utter confidence, as the lover and saviour of Judah. He urged every king who reigned during his lifetime to put his trust in God rather than in allies.

189 What happened as a result?

Having driven Merodach-Baladan from his throne, and having turned to the Palestinian states, Sennacherib was not long in arriving before the walls of Jerusalem. He had known full well of the intrigues between Hezekiah and the Babylonians and was determined to teach the Judeans a lesson they would never forget. Jerusalem was quickly reduced to the last extremity, and Hezekiah only saved himself and his city by the payment of an indemnity that left it stripped and bare.

190 Was Judah saved?

Immediately upon gathering up the loot, the Assyrians started to leave, apparently intending to make another foray into Egypt. They had not gone far when Sennacherib repented of having left so strong a fortress intact on his flank, and an army was sent back to reduce it. The Assyrians, flushed with victory, appeared before the walls of the city with jeers, ridiculing the defenders' confidence in Yahweh (II Kings 18:19-25; 19:10-13). At this point Isaiah entered the scene in his last great climactic act.

191 What had Isaiah been doing?

He had been bitterly opposed to Judah's part in the revolt (Isaiah 1:4-7); but when Hezekiah's emissaries reported the ridicule of Yahweh mouthed by the Assyrians Isaiah took an entirely different attitude, counseling resistance and putting himself at the king's disposal. His proffer of help was accepted, and therewith he became, and continued until the king's death, the equivalent of prime minister (II Kings 19:3-7).

192 What was the outcome?

The forces surrounded the city for a period of time without making any direct assault. Then one night something happened, the exact nature of which will never be known. Some say that an invasion of field mice gnawed the bowstrings of the army, leaving them unarmed and helpless. Others say that a plague broke out among them. At any rate, they fled in disorder and the city was saved. Hezekiah was won over completely to the prophetic party, and Isaiah began praching the indestructibility of Jerusalem openly.

193 Was Isaiah entirely absorbed in political matters?

Throughout his long career politics absorbed the major part of his interest because the political destiny of the nation was so intimately wrapped up in his life and that of his countrymen. He was equally interested in social and moral reform because they contributed to any political success. He preached against the prevailing alcoholism of his time with power and earnestness (Isaiah 28:7-8). He castigated officers of the government without mercy (28:14-22) because he believed their immorality exposed the nation to grave dangers. With all the indignation of a highborn gentleman he rebuked the lowborn for their boorishness. He was in every sense as militant as Amos in his defense of the poor and his condemnation of those injustices which broke the hearts of the people (3:13-15). Against the widespread immorality he was equally vehement (5:11, 20, 22-23; 10:1-2).

194 How was Isaiah accepted by the religious leaders?

In the estimation of the religious leaders he was more politician than preacher. Isaiah, in turn, held the priests and professional prophets up to scorn (1:10-20). Though he was intensely religious, Isaiah always considered himself a layman without formal or professional religious connections.

195 Was all his preaching political?

In a sense it was. He preached that all wickedness on the part of individuals was sure to have its effect in weakening the nation. He appealed for righteousness that the nation might be saved, for righteousness was to him the highest patriotism.

196 Was Isaiah a world preacher?

Not in the sense that Amos was. He saw the Assyrian Empire as a monstrous thing (10:16-19; 14:24-27) which Yahweh was using as an instrument for disciplining Judah (10:5-6), but he never held out any hope that Assyria herself could be saved if she became penitent.

197 When did Isaiah's career end?

No one knows. There is an old tradition to the effect that he died a martyr during the reactionary reign of Manasseh, who succeeded Hezekiah, but of this we have no direct knowledge. With the retreat of Sennacherib from before the walls of

Jerusalem Isaiah passes from the scene and we hear nothing more from him.

198 Who was Micah?

He was a countryman from one of the villages southwest of Jerusalem. The city of Gath had been a Philistine stronghold back in the days of Saul and David, and had given its name to an entire section of the country. The little village of Moresheth was one of a number of small settlements in the district, which explains the fact that Micah describes it as "Moresheth-gath." Nothing remains today of any of the villages, but they are known to have been situated about midway between Jerusalem and Gaza. Located on the top of low-lying hills, they skirted the great caravan routes along which the Assyrians marched as they went down to plunder Egypt. The people of these villages were as a consequence greatly interested in the international situation, for if war came to Judah the region of Gath would be first to feel the blows.

Micah's father is not mentioned, which indicates that he belonged to the poorer class; and it is reasonable to assume that he was one of those dispossessed who had suffered much under the administration of the wealthy landlords of Jerusalem. At least he did not belong to the aristocracy, and certainly he did not belong in any city. Like Amos, Micah was a man of the people, and with all the fury of an impassioned soul he struck out against the evils and injustices under which they suffered.

199 When did he preach?

It is impossible to fix the date precisely, for he mentions no kings, event, or circumstance which will serve as a basis for reckoning. The first verse of his book suggests the general period; further evidence in the book leads to the conclusion that he began preaching about 725 B.C., during the last year of Ahaz; and a single reference to the sacrifices of children (Micah 6:6-8) would give reason to believe that the period was that of Manasseh, who succeeded Hezekiah, coming to the throne in 696 B.C.

200 Where did Micah preach?

The only town named is that of his home community, but

because the Hebrews made frequent trips to the Temple in Jerusalem it is safe to assume that Micah was a more or less frequent visitor there. Jeremiah, a hundred years later, hints that he had been there (Jeremiah 26:17-19), and it is not unreasonable to assume that he had preached in the capital. Generally speaking, however, Micah is thought of as a country preacher in contrast to Isaiah, whose ministry occurred in Jerusalem.

201   What were the political conditions of the times?

The long-threatened Assyrian invasion was actually in progress, and to the vandalism of the invaders along the seacoast Micah must have been a witness. In 732 B.C. the city of Damascus, capital of Syria, fell to Tiglath Pileser, and the last barrier to the invasion of the Hebrew kingdoms was removed. In his lifetime Micah saw Israel in the throes of civil war, invaded by Assyria, compelled to pay tribute, reduced to complete vassalage, and finally destroyed as a nation. As a helpless onlooker from the low hills of Judah he had watched her come to her pitiful end, with the gloomy predictions of Amos and Hosea fulfilled before his eyes. In the meantime (732 B.C.) tribute was being extorted from Judah; and Micah, as a poor countryman upon whom the burden fell heaviest, was painfully familiar with all the suffering which attended this process. His sermons were preached during one of the most heartbreaking periods in Hebrew history, at a time when a terrible doom hung over all the world.

202   Why did the tax burden fall heaviest on country-men?

The tribute was assessed against the nation, but the demand for each year's payment was made upon the government at Jerusalem. It mattered little to Assyria how the money was collected, so long as it was forthcoming. The rich nobles and officials in Jerusalem simply passed the burden on, requiring the country districts to furnish quotas. When these quotas had been paid it was discovered that enough had been collected to meet the bill, and the city landowners were left untouched. All this was well known throughout the kingdom, but the people were helpless to defend themselves. It was against this system that all the eighth-century prophets protested.

203 What were the religious conditions of the times?

The conditions described as prevailing in Isaiah's time were those of Micah's time, for they were contemporaries.

204 Did Isaiah and Micah work together?

It is interesting to note that Micah 4:1-3 also appears in Isaiah 2:2-4, but no one knows which borrowed from the other or whether both borrowed from some unknown prophet. That Micah was familiar with some of Isaiah's ideas also seems to be true (compare Micah 2:1-5 with Isaiah 5:8-10 and Micah 3:3 with Isaiah 3:15), but aside from this fragmentary evidence we have no way of knowing that they co-operated in any way.

205 Was Micah known to Amos or Hosea?

Both Micah and Amos were Judeans from the same general area, but Amos preached in Israel. Though it is possible that Micah had heard about Amos we have no hint anywhere in the Bible that this was true. There is, however, some similarity between Micah 2:6 and Amos 2:12 and 7:13. There seems to have been no contact whatever between Micah and Hosea.

206 Was Micah informed on the political situation?

From the hilltops just east of the great caravan route over which Sargon led his hosts, Micah had watched the destruction of villages and towns. Among them perhaps had been his own village of Moresheth-gath. This had familiarized him with the tragedy and suffering of the plain people of the rural districts (Micah 1:10-14). To Micah it appeared that the affliction which was being visited upon Samaria reached clear up to the gates of Jerusalem (1:9). It was as if he were saying, "We are all in this thing together." And the blame for it all he laid at the doors of the princes and priests—the Jerusalem nobility. Because the rich and propertied classes had sinned against the poor, he professed to see the whole nation doomed to unutterable woes.

207 What did he call sins?

Micah saw the whole problem of Judah centering in the question of *mishpat*—the social and economic systems of justice. The land question was especially important to him (2:1-2), for it seemed to him that the wealthy schemers must lie awake nights devising plans by which they could seize farms and homes. Pious pretenders advised the prophets to stick to religion and not to meddle in economic matters (2:6), and the prophet esteemed them no better than night prowlers (2:8), greedy cannibals (3:3), and exploiters of women and children (2:9). As he surveyed the scene he was convinced that all the leading citizens were corrupt (6:9), with the false prophets playing to the crowds (3:5, 11) in their professionalism. The courts perverted justice (3:1, 5; 7:3) and the big cities were the source of all their woes (6:9; 3:12).

208 Why did Micah condemn the cities?

From the days of the Hebrew occupation of the land the exploiters and paganizers had centered in the cities. Canaanite in their philosophy of life and religion, the cities had remained the seat of the powerful. With the government centralized in the capital, it was perfectly natural that Jerusalem should have become the gathering place for the rich and the powerful. Micah seems to have thought of Jerusalem much as the modern small-town businessman, laborer, or farmer thinks of "Wall Street." The influences that flowed out from the capital dominated the economic, social, political, and religious life of the entire nation.

209 Was sin confined to the cities?

By no means. It spread all over the nation. But about twenty-five years previous to the ministry of Micah an economic and social revolution had set in throughout Judah and Israel, as we have seen, which had as serious effect upon the life of the people as did the Industrial Revolution on the lives of the English. There was immorality in the rural areas, of course, but the unjust social system which was weighing so heavily upon the country people stemmed from Jerusalem. To Micah it appeared a fact that all the forces which were undermining the ancient *mishpat* originated in Jerusalem. It was against the sinful systems rather than sinful individuals that Micah preached.

210 Did Micah preach no personal message of religion?

There is very little personal religion in Micah's book. He says nothing about personal immorality, personal salvation, or personal communion with God. He does describe the way in which devout men must approach Yahweh (6:8), but it is not offered as advice on the subject of how to "save one's soul."

211 What was Micah's judgment upon the nation?

He saw the people debased by social injustices and economic wrongs. He recognized the fact that for every wrong there was a corresponding spiritual and moral loss. He did not believe it was possible to have the approval of Yahweh upon the nation if it visited unjust conditions upon the people. While Micah spoke he had the bent backs and haggard faces of the poor before his eyes. Pinched and starved folk peered up at him and begged him to make their cause his own as he preached to the nation.

212 Did he have the support of the religious leaders?

The religious leaders were the professional prophets who preached glibly and pleasantly according to the way they were fed. They lived off the alms of the rich and flattered them accordingly. The professional prophet spoke, consciously or unconsciously, for himself and his living. He did not attack the sins of his day, and that was what made him a false prophet (3:5-7). Against all such Micah cried out with great vehemence, and it is natural to assume that he aroused the enmity of those whose easy livings he imperiled.

213 Did Micah oppose the government?

It is important to notice that he spoke no word against the king. Hezekiah, the monarch who sat upon the throne in Judah, enjoyed a good reputation and was one of the more enlightened rulers. It was the rich and powerful nobles who hung about the courts and constituted the political machine in Jerusalem who were the targets of his shafts. Judges, priests, and prophets were all alike mercenary. The city of Jerusalem, he said, was built with blood, and no walls could stand on such foundations.

214 Was all this religious?

It depends upon the definition we give to the word "religious." If we are thinking in terms of personal religion,

76

with its emphasis on repentance, conversion, faith divine guidance, forgiveness, heaven, immortality, and other ideas in contemporaneous religious discussions, then there cannot be said to be much "religion" in Micah's book. But as we think of religion as meaning a domination of all of life with the thought of a just and holy God, with a summoning of every interest and activity of life before him for judgment, then the book of Micah is of the very essence of religion. Micah believed that the social and economic conditions in Judah were an offense to Yahweh, and that the nation would suffer as an inevitable consequence.

215 Did the war affect Micah's preaching?

It did for Micah exactly what the threat of war does to preachers anywhere, for he could not be indifferent to the greatest problem the people faced.

216 What did Micah have to say about the situation?

He blamed the nation's leaders, saying that it was their sins that had involved the country in such terrible danger. He saw the terror descending upon a wicked and evil nation (6:9-16), guilty of short weights, idolatry, terrorism, exploitation, and a long list of other crimes. Charging first Israel (1:5) and then Judah (1:8-9) with sin, he protested with all his powers. The doom that overhung the little kingdoms he believed to be the natural and inevitable fruitage of their sins.

217 How did the fall of Samaria come about?

Three things helped the little kingdom to resist the mighty Empire: (1) The Assyrians were plainsmen who had lived all their lives in level country. They had learned to fight on the plains, in masses. Palestine was a mountainous country, and the Hebrews had learned to fight in such a land. The techniques of the two styles of warfare were very different. In the mountains the fighting is individualistic. Fifty or twenty strong men could hold a pass against a large number of enemies, or a few hundred men fighting from the hilltops could work havoc with a host of men marching at the bottom of the canyons. It was always easy to construct ambushes. (2) The Palestinians were fighting for their homes and the Assyrians were fighting for loot, with the psychology of the situation altogether in favor of the invaded. (3) Assyria had other enemies. Her empire was always loosely organized and revolts were springing up in the rear at all times. This necessitated frequent withdrawals of troops, sometimes on the very eve of an attack. Eleven times in one hundred years the Assyrians arrived at the borders of Israel, only to be driven off. This always gave the Hebrews confidence that it would happen again. Up to Micah's time there had been some reason for listening to the warnings of the prophets with contempt, but in his day the case was entirely different. The enemies in the rear were subdued and reduced to impotency. A powerful king was in command of a well-equipped army whose morale was high. The fall of Damascus and Samaria and the imminent fall of Judah were facts not to be ignored. Only a miracle could save them. In the case of Damascus and Samaria no miracle occurred, and no miracle could be counted on to save Judah.

218 Did Micah understand all this?

He could hardly have failed to know the general situation, for Samaria was less than fifty miles from Moresheth-gath, and messengers raced away in every direction with the news. Micah lived only a mile or two from a crowded trade route where all the world went by with the news.

219 Was not Micah prejudiced?

Being a countryman, he may have been prejudiced against the cities; but the rich and powerful merchants and capitalists of Jerusalem and other cities had so organized their business that the plain people bore the brunt of the injustices, and Micah was one of those who knew from first-hand experience how the system worked. Therefore he raised his voice in a mighty protest; and in this he will rank as one of the greatest battlers against economic and social injustices of all times, even though he never heard the word economic or social and knew no difference between "sacred" and "secular." He judged the day in which he lived by its effect upon the lives of the common people, and that effect he believed to be unspeakably bad.

220 Was Micah's voice the only one raised?

The religious leaders were all silent about the sins which

Micah condemned. Priests and prophets alike were guilty of practicing graft (3:9-11). False prophets encouraged the nation in its sins because they had no spiritual vision to enable them to see its sinfulness.

221 **What effect did his preaching have upon the nation?**

No more than any other preacher of doom may expect. He was able to arouse neither penitence nor fear. The land-grabbing went on (2:1-5), and some even called him a blasphemer (2:6-7), preferring prophets who preached pleasant and comfortable sermons (2:8-11). But with the passing of the years his influence mounted, so that a hundred years afterward when Jeremiah was in the midst of one of his most difficult experiences a quotation from Micah was sufficient to save him (Jeremiah 26:16-19).

222 **Did Micah and Isaiah agree?**

Isaiah, it will be remembered, taught that Jerusalem would stand eternally because Yahweh needed it as the visible evidence of earthly rule (Isaiah 29:7-8); but Micah declared that the nation was doomed because it had sinned against *mishpat* (Micah 3:9-12). Though the two disagreed on the fate of Jerusalem, they agreed in their diagnosis of the nation's woes. The entire blame for the impending disasters was rooted in the economic and moral offenses against *mishpat*.

223 **What is the final judgment on these four prophets?**

The great writing prophets of the eighth century B.C. were all the product of their times. Confronted with perils that were the fruitage of the first great world crisis, interpreting their times in terms of their faith, preaching the will of God as it had been revealed to them, profoundly convinced that their words had been given to them by Yahweh, they have made themselves immortal. But it must never be forgotten that they were men of the eighth century, immersed in practical problems, speaking with the confidence that they were divinely guided, and saying those things which, because of their truthfulness, are of permanent value to those who seek to know and to do the will of God in every area of life.

224 What is the modern significance of the first world crisis?

Devout men, divinely guided, found their way through the awful experiences of a world collapse to divine truth. The little kingdoms of Israel and Judah have completely disappeared. The great empires—Assyria and Egypt—are fields for archaeological study, with their great cities standing as age-long ruins. But the sublime truths preached by the Hebrew prophets are still as radiant and as creative as the day they were first uttered, and the great treasure that has come down to us from that ancient day is embedded in their words.